The PASSION of CHRIST

Martin Luther

The Passion of Christ
© 2020 by Martin Luther
Gideon House Books

ISBN: 978-1-943133-82-6

Scripture quotations taken from
The Holy Bible, New International Version® NIV®
Copyright © 1973 1978 1984 2011 by Biblica, Inc.™
Used by permission. All rights reserved worldwide.

Cover design and interior layout by
Josh Pritchard

GIDEON HOUSE BOOKS
www.gideonhousebooks.com

CONTENTS

Introductory Meditations 5

1. The Occurrences at the Mount of Olives 19
2. The Seizure of Christ in the Garden 31
3. Christ Refusing to be Rescued by Peter's Sword 43
4. The Lord Jesus Led to Annas and Caiaphas and Tried by the Jews..53
5. Peter Thrice Denies the Lord Jesus in the House of Caiaphas 61
6. Christ is Delivered to Pilate.—Judas Hangs Himself. —The Potter's Field...71
7. Christ Accused before Pilate and Condemned to Death 85
8. Explanation of Several Points in the History just Given 93
9. Christ Led away to be Crucified.—Simon Bears the Cross after Him.—The Women who Follow Bewail and Lament Him...103
10. Christ Nailed to the Cross—His Deeds, Sufferings and Words on the Cross.. 115
11. Christ's Prayer on the Cross.—The Malefactor on the Right............127
12. Christ Commits His Mother to the Care of John. —The Soldiers do not Break the Legs of Christ, but with a Spear Pierce His Side, from which Blood and Water Flow 139
13. Christ's Body Taken down from the Cross and Laid in a Tomb. —The Soldiers Guard the Tomb 153

INTRODUCTORY MEDITATIONS

In this season of the year it is customary for the Church, both in her hymns and sermons, to dwell especially upon the passion of Christ. We also will follow this custom. Indeed, we consider it very appropriate that the narrative of the sufferings of our Lord should, at a certain fixed period of the year, be read in the churches to the people, word for word, from beginning to end, and that it be fully explained to them, so that they may understand its use, and derive from it much consolation. It is sadly evident with what effect the devil resists the Gospel, though it be preached daily, and how the hearts grow cold towards it, so that they do not amend, but rather grow worse from year to year. This distressing fact ought surely to prompt us to continue in the preaching of the Word, and especially of that part of it which tells of the suffering and death of Christ. We must endeavor to have the people know and appreciate this part of the Gospel; nor dare we be derelict in the performance of this duty. If we would neglect to preach on this subject one, two or three years, the people would surely forget it. Even we, who continually busy ourselves with the Word, experience a decrease of interest in it if we neglect the perusal of it for a day or two; how great then would be the injury to the people at large, if they should miss the preaching of these truths for a year or two? They would become as wild as beasts; therefore it is so urgent that we preach and teach the Word in season and out of season. The devil is ever active in resisting the efficacy of the Word, else there would be many believers, and people would be converted; for surely it is now preached often and clearly.

For the Papists this week is one of torture; they sing and read and preach exceedingly much concerning the passion of Christ. But what does it avail them? It is true, they speak of Christ's sufferings; but in their heart there is no thought of them, or else they would not prize so highly their own self-inflicted penances and their own works. But it is not much better with us, who have the pure Gospel abundantly preached to us; our lives and deeds indicate that we also have disregarded it. The effects of the preaching of the Word are therefore not the same with all, inasmuch as not all are disposed to receive it. If we were to relate to the people some idle tales and stories, they would remember them at once; whereas now, thousands upon thousands hear repeatedly the preaching of the Gospel without retaining it, and without profiting by its instructions. They come back from church just as they went there. They hear the Word, but disregard it as something common and unimportant.

There are some, on the other hand, who hear it gladly when they are told Christ rendered satisfaction for us, and that by our own merits and works we cannot obtain salvation, but that Christ alone has purchased it for us by His sufferings and death; but as soon as they are told that to enjoy the benefits of this atonement they must avoid avarice, worldly-mindedness, gluttony, self-esteem, &c., they are displeased and become enraged. They are unwilling to be rebuked on account of their sins, or to be regarded as Gentiles. Here, also, it is the devil who labors to make the Word of no effect, and we cannot expect any thing else but such aversion to the application of the truth. It behooves us so much the more, to continue steadfast in the Word, to the glory of God and to our own souls' salvation, that some may learn to love it, although many are indifferent, and that thus the sacrifice of the Son of God in our behalf may be known and remembered.

The preaching of this truth began in Paradise, when it was said to Adam and Eve that the seed of the woman should crush the head of the serpent. The Church has retained the proclamation of this Gospel, and will retain it until the end of time. Nor can we perform any better service than to proclaim everywhere, in the church, from the pulpit and at home, this fact of the sacrifice of God for the redemption of all mankind.

As Israel was heavily burdened with the ceremonial law, and was compelled to sacrifice calves, heifers, &c., thus the papacy still conducts its divine worship. If we had to observe all those ceremonies and defray all the expenses incident to them, I fear there would be many complaints of insufferable burdens. But not much is required of us: only this pleasing service, that we should remember His boundless mercy, manifested in the sacrifice of His Son for our sins, and that we should preach this and teach it to our children. Let us thank God it we can enjoy such divine service, which surely will not be useless, but will rather bring forth glorious fruits and many blessings unto men.

The Turks have lost this kind of worship; they have forgotten Christ and substituted Mahomet in His place. The Jews have also rejected Him. Nor is it much better in Germany, where people have become weary of this worship and neglect it. But we may depend upon it that as soon as this true worship is lost, so soon will punishment follow. If we refuse to worship God, when we need only to hear a sermon which tells us of the suffering and death of Christ for us, we need look for nothing else but that, as a well merited penalty, another more severe, and withal an ineffective kind of worship will be imposed upon us. Therefore we ought to preach and hear, right willingly, of the passion of our Lord, so that we may never forget its blessings, even though Satan, the old enemy of truth, may busily attempt to resist and crush the Word.

But again, our own wants require that this be done. As long as we live in this world our flesh and blood will burden us, even as would the weight of a millstone. On every side we are subjected to temptations which take possession of our thoughts and time, so that we forget Christ and His sufferings; earthly possessions, worldly honor, food, drink, carnal indulgences, misfortunes, sickness and adversity are all, more or less, apt to have such an effect upon us. Hence it is necessary to set apart an especial season for the service of God. The devil is ever on the alert to insinuate all kinds of wickedness into our hearts, and would fain make them as cold as ice. Where God's Word is not repeatedly proclaimed in sermons, in hymns, in private conversation, so that we may not forget it or become callous towards it, there it is impossible for our hearts, which are burdened with many an earthly pain and sorrow, with wicked purposes and the devil's malicious instigations, not to fail and to fall from Christ. Thus it is an urgent necessity that the preaching of the Gospel continue among us, that we may hear and retain it, otherwise we would soon forget our Lord.

Nor should we overlook the wants of our young people, who need instruction so much; and many mechanics, laborers, and servants, who are Christians by baptism, cannot even read. Much zeal and energy is needed, that these people may be taught that which they know not, but which is so important to their welfare. God cannot be satisfied with us, if we disregard the precious treasure which He has given us; if we, perhaps, hear the preaching of the Word and gape at it without learning anything. Nor will the devil desist from his attempts to cause us to do what is evil. If we will not hear, nor learn, nor remember the word of truth, we will be condemned to listen to and heed the falsehoods of the devil, unto our souls' eternal damnation. The Papists, the Turks, the Jews, and Anabaptists are examples of this. Let us, therefore, never grow weary of the proper worship of God; let us readily hear and heed the sermons preached on the passion of Christ.

The Benefits Accruing from the Passion of Christ

Of these St. Paul in his Epistle to the Romans, 5 chap., thus writes: "But God commendeth His love toward us, in that, while we were yet sinners, Christ died for us. Much more then, being now justified by His blood, we shall be saved from wrath through Him. For if, when we were enemies, we were reconciled to God by the death of His Son, much more, being reconciled, we shall be saved by His life. And not only so, but we also joy in God through our Lord Jesus Christ, by whom we have now received the atonement."

To preach the passion of Christ our Lord properly, it is not sufficient to read the narrative to the people, but we must add admonition and instruction, that they may realize and remember why Christ suffered thus, and in what way they are benefited by His passion. The method pursued by the Papists, especially by the monks, in presenting this truth, and which was only calculated to arouse the emotions of the people and to fill them with pity and lamentation, must be rejected as utterly useless. He who could stir up the emotions of people best was considered the most effective passion-preacher. Hence we find in those sermons principally railing against the Jews, descriptions of the lamentation of the Virgin Mary when she saw the death of her Son, and the like. All this, however, is nothing but hypocrisy, as really all worship in the papacy is; the true spirit of devotion is wanting, and there are no fruits of amendment there. If we attentively consider the preaching of the apostles and prophets, we shall find a totally different method of preaching on the passion of our Lord. They did not waste words on the simple story of the event, but presented it unadorned, pointedly and briefly. But of the meaning of this passion, and how it is effective for us if properly applied,—of this they spake repeatedly and much.

It was indeed a short sermon, if merely the words are counted, when John spake of Christ: "Behold the Lamb of God, which taketh away the sin of the world;" but if we carefully meditate upon these words, we will discover how much they contain for our edification and comfort, if we but receive them in true faith.

John calls the Lord a "Lamb," because He was to be slain, even as a victim is slain. All the sacrifices of heifers, oxen, calves and lambs, which took place under the Old Testament, were but types of that perfect and only efficient sacrifice, which Christ our Saviour offered to redeem the whole world through His own blood. To this the Evangelist refers in the above words, in which he dwells but incidentally upon the narrative of the passion itself. He calls Christ not merely a lamb, but "the Lamb of God," to express thereby the truth that God Himself had instituted this sacrifice, and would be well pleased with it. This expression, "Lamb of God," is further intended to arouse our faith to accept such a sacrifice, which God in His infinite mercy and love has made for our salvation. Yea, by it we are to be convinced that because God Himself ordained this sacrifice, it is really perfect and all-sufficient to accomplish what these words say, namely, to take away the sin of the world. In this expression, "sin of the world," is included all impiety and injustice which prevail in the world, and which cause the dreadful, but just wrath of God. Now all this wrong God has in mercy taken from the world, and has imposed it upon His Son, who paid our debt for us, that we might be exempt from fear and punishment.

We learn from this example how to preach rightly on the passion of Christ. We should not dwell chiefly upon the historical incidents connected with it, such as the betrayal, the scourging, the mockery, and the crucifixion of Christ; all this we ought to know and to preach; but this is not the most important lesson of the passion of Christ. Above all we must know and believe, as John preaches, that Christ suffered on account of our sins, which God cast upon Him, and which He bore in obedience to His Father's will and from love toward us. If we know this; if we understand our sinful condition, which would have plunged us without escape into eternal damnation, had not Christ become our Saviour, we will duly appreciate the importance and value of the suffering of our Lord, and will be comforted thereby when fear of God's wrath, on account of our sins, would overcome us. Such a consideration of the passion of Christ will not only move our eyes to tears and our hearts to pity, as is the tendency of the popish sermons on this subject, but will prompt us to feel, deep down in our soul, sorrow at the terrible results of sin, for which no creature, but only the Son of God could make atonement by His sufferings and death; and likewise it will cause us great joy, because we will realize that this sacrifice was made for us, that God will now no longer reject nor condemn us, as we have merited by our sins, but that He is now reconciled to us through the precious and vicarious death of His Son, who gave Himself as a victim in our behalf, so that our sins are now forgiven and we are made heirs of eternal life.

The Papists never preached thus of the passion of Christ. They also used the words "Lamb of God" as applied to Christ who took away the sin of the world, but their whole worship was arranged as if each individual had to bear his own sin and must make atonement for it himself. How else can we understand the stringent regulation in the Romish Church, especially in this season of the year, in regard to fastings, penances, self-inflicted tortures and other severe and burdensome works? Why were people so much in terror in regard to the minute, outward confession of their sins? Why did they bury themselves day and night in the churches and chapels, engaging in song and prayers? Was it not because they supposed that by such doings and observances they could and must work out forgiveness of their sins? Such doings mean in reality that we cannot rely, fully and solely, upon the sacrifice of Christ as all-sufficient and effective, and that we must with our own work complete the sacrifice and the atonement.

This contradicts directly the statement of John the Baptist, yea of Christ Himself, when in John 12. He thus speaks of His sufferings: "The hour is come that the Son of man should be glorified. Verily, verily, I say unto you, except a corn of wheat fall into the ground and die, it abideth alone: but if it die, it bringeth forth much fruit." In these words Christ declares that His sufferings shall abound in much fruit. It would be erroneous to claim that the Christian must first of all bring forth good works, even as the branch and the vine bringeth forth grapes; this would indeed be one of the fruits of union with Christ through faith, but the most important fruit is indicated in the words of the Lord Himself when He says: "And I, if I be lifted up from the earth, will draw all men unto me;" that is, through me, through my sacrifice, through my death upon the cross, men must come to the Father and receive eternal life. They who rely on their own works, and desire by means of them to enter heaven, pervert the plan of salvation; they draw Christ down to them, whereas the reverse should take place. Christ must draw us to Him, or everything is lost. He alone has vanquished the devil, paid the penalty of our sins, rescued us from the world and death, and brought us to life through His sufferings and death. To all this we contributed nothing.

Again, John 3. chapter, Christ preaches of His passion in this wise: "And as Moses lifted up the serpent in the wilderness, even so must the Son of man be lifted up: that whosoever believeth in Him should not perish, but have eternal life." This is sufficiently plain. Whosoever desires to have eternal life, must obtain it through faith in Christ and His death upon the cross, wherewith He made payment for our sins and redeemed us from death and hell. In the words just cited, Christ mentions no work of man as efficient unto justification; He says nothing of alms, fastings and the like. The requirement of deeds came already through Moses, and in the ten commandments God laid down the rules of conduct to be observed by us, and whosoever disregards them may expect the wrath of God and His punishments. He, however, who keeps the law, and fulfills its demands as much as he can, does not on that account get to heaven. There was no other remedy for the Jews in the wilderness, when bitten by the fiery serpents, but to look up to the brazen serpent which God had ordered to be made. In like manner, as Christ indicates in this passage, there is no other way unto salvation but faithfully to look unto Him who sacrificed Himself, according to the will of God, for our sins, and through whom we now have pardon and eternal life. Such a glorious result has the death of Christ; our works do not accomplish it, as the Papists falsely teach; they have nothing to do with it.

The prophets also frequently speak similar words. Thus Isaiah, 53. chapter, says: "Surely he hath borne our griefs, and carried our sorrows: yet we did esteem Him stricken, smitten of God and afflicted. But He was wounded for our transgressions, He was bruised for our iniquities: the chastisement of our peace was upon Him; and with His stripes we are healed." Surely, this is a most charming and comfortable passion-sermon, yea no apostle in the New Testament could preach one to surpass it. The prophet declares that Christ shall be stricken, smitten and afflicted in our behalf, and also that the chastisement of our peace shall be upon Him, and that with His stripes we are to be healed. Isaiah calls the Lord a physician, and directs us to Him to be healed in our distress and sickness, so that we may obtain health and happiness. The Lord has a remedy for us which is not labeled good works, giving of alms, fastings and rosaries, but consists of the fact that He suffered and died for us, yea, that He bore our griefs and carried our sorrows. If therefore the history of the passion tells us how our blessed Lord and Saviour was tortured by the Jews and the Gentiles, we ought to be mindful that all this happened that we, even we, might have a cure, not from bodily infirmities, but from a sickness more dreadful than all the rest, namely, from sin and eternal death. Thus the history of the passion will be applied by us properly and happily. It must, however, be borne in mind that the passion of Christ is in two ways a precious and sure remedy. It exhibits, in the first place, sin in all its ugliness and terror; no human being, not an angel, nor any other created being, had the power to take away sin; the Son of God alone could do it, and He did carry this crushing weight for us. We should therefore carefully and earnestly endeavor to avoid sin, in the fear of God, for it is so very easy to fall into it, and so very difficult to get out of it again. In this endeavor we will be mightily assisted by the consideration of the passion of Christ, which will prompt us, as a precious power against sin, to be pious and to shun evil, since it is such a terrible and dreadful burden, which no created being can remove, and which the Son of God had to carry for us. In the second place, we find in the passion of Christ a rescue from death; for he who fully believes that the Son of God died for his sins and paid his debt before God, can have a peaceful heart and need not fear death, but will trust in the mercy of God and hope for eternal salvation. Of this consolation the prophet prisoners out of the pit wherein is no water. Turn you to the stronghold ye prisoners of hope," &c. The pit, the prison-house of men, is sin and its punishments, namely, the tyranny of the devil and eternal death. From this pit we could not rescue ourselves unless by the help of God; not through the blood of heifers and similar victims, but only through the blood of the just One, the King of Salvation. He who is not in the covenant of this blood must remain in the pit of sin and eternal death, while he who is enrolled in it through faith shall surely come out from this pit of wrath to the enjoyment of the mercy of God and unto eternal life.

Daniel also preaches of this, in the 9. chapter: "Seventy weeks are determined upon Thy people and upon Thy holy city, to finish the transgression, and to make an end of sin, and to make reconciliation for iniquity, and to bring in everlasting righteousness," &c. How this should be fulfilled in the death of Christ, the prophet soon after indicates. This is another clear and definite declaration of the truth, that forgiveness of sins and justification can be obtained only through the death of Jesus Christ; through it, if we accept it in faith, we have this precious treasure, and in no other way can we obtain it. Thus we can learn from John the Baptist, from Christ Himself, and from the prophets, how to preach of the passion of our Lord, namely, to instruct the hearts as to the mercy and grace of God, that they may be comforted thereby. Christ suffered for the payment of our sins, to reconcile us to God, and to save us through faith in Him as our Lord and Saviour.

The holy Apostles preached the same truth concerning the passion of Christ, as we can easily read in their narratives and writings. Of the many passages bearing upon this point we will now, in conclusion, notice but the one taken from Romans 5. chapter, as you, my beloved, have heard it in the beginning of this discourse. This passage is sufficiently plain, so that all can understand it. Nevertheless we will now dwell upon it somewhat, to our instruction, edification and comfort.

We all experience how deeply unbelief is rooted in our hearts, so that we are ever troubled by our sins, and lack all assurance and peace. We are so ready to exclaim: Ah, if we were only more pious, it would be better for us, and we could then hope for the mercy of God. Where the heart thus wavers, there is surely trepidation and uneasiness. But if we firmly believe, and rely on the mercy of God, which He has promised in Christ, our hearts will be securely stayed in all adversities upon this consolation, and will indeed be happy and of good cheer.

People, however, are perverse in this. The Pope has therefore established all manner of worship, by means of which, as he pretends, confidence in God and reliance on His help can be gained. Some of these inventions are worship of the saints, pilgrimages, the purchase of indulgences, the mass, vigils, monastic life, and other similar delusions. Such observances are regarded as guarantees of a renewed life and of heaven. This is indeed a deep-rooted delusion, and an earnest preacher of the truth will direct his efforts chiefly against it, to tear from the hearts of the people, by the grace of God, this wicked unbelief and to instill into them true confidence and faith. How to do this properly, and with success, St. Paul teaches us in the passage under consideration; and, surely, his testimony is of great weight, as of one who was a great preacher, chosen and called of God Himself as a giant in the work of spreading the Gospel. We ought, therefore, attentively to heed his words.

He begins with the remark: "God commendeth his love toward us," which is indeed a peculiar and astonishing saying, but nevertheless, as we shall presently hear, a remarkable, precious truth. God, it is true, is the declared enemy of sin, and will punish it, as the law demands and as our daily experience proves. Again, it is true that we are all sinners, and this knowledge causes our unbelief of the mercy and love of God. When told, as in the passage before us, that God loves man, we think immediately of John the Baptist, of Peter, of Paul and others, who were so much more pious than we, and are ready to admit that God may love such as these, but we deny that we are such people as He can love, and therefore continue in fear of His wrath. Against this misconception the Apostle directs his words when he says that God doth not only love us, but that He even commendeth His love toward us; that is, God makes it so manifest, so sure and evident that He loves us, that no man can doubt it. What else but love could prompt Him to send His only begotten Son, Jesus Christ, into this world, to die for us while we were yet sinners? When therefore sin and doubt torment us, and would rob us of confidence in God's mercy and pardon, let us firmly hold to the eternal truth of this word: "While we were yet sinners Christ died for us." Who is Christ? He is the Son of God. What does He do? He becomes man and dies. Why does He die? On account of sinners. From this it clearly follows that God has not rejected sinners, and that He desires not their destruction, but that He loves them still, even so much that He rescues them from sin and death. For their sake His dear Son goes into death by the will of the Father. What better proof of His love could He have given? Surely, St. Paul has good authority for exclaiming: "God commendeth His love toward us;" and it behooves us to confess the precious, inexhaustible grace of God in Christ, and to believe that He is no longer wroth with us. Indeed, it would be utter madness to say that God will cast us away in anger, when it is evident that He gave His only begotten Son as a sacrifice for us wicked and forlorn men, that we might be redeemed, and have salvation evermore.

These words of St. Paul agree fully with the saying of Christ, John 3: "For God so loved the world, that He gave His only begotten Son, that whosoever believeth in Him should not perish, but have everlasting life." How can one, who knows and believes that God loves him, be afraid of Him? For we all know what the character of love is. It is not contentious nor injurious, but trusts in Him, to whom it is directed, convinced that He will bring help and assistance. It is impossible to be otherwise. We should therefore cultivate this love, and fondly cherish it, nor permit any one or any thing to rob us of it. It is the devil's especial aim to persuade or force us from this conviction that God loves us; he would fain have us fear God and regard Him as our deadly enemy. Where he succeeds in this attempt he has won the field. If we have lost our confidence in God, what then can defend or support us? Let us therefore resolutely repel all such insinuations of the devil, of sin and our conscience, as if God did not love us, but let us firmly hold to the eternal truth and consolation that, as an assurance of His love, God sent His Son into this world to die for us sinners—to save us even while we were yet sinners. What else is this but a proof that God has thoughts of mercy toward sinners, that He loves them and would help them from their misery? This consolation we derive, as St. Paul here tells us, from the death and passion of Christ, and we should be comforted thereby. When the knowledge of our sins depresses us, when our heart would question the mercy and favor of God, we should be quick to conclude that He cannot be our enemy, since He gave us His only begotten Son as a Saviour. Hence we dare assuredly depend upon His mercy and help, and have no cause of fear or despair.

But perhaps you will say: we know well enough that God gave His Son into death in our behalf, yet we, on our part, have by many transgressions and sins proved ourselves totally unworthy of this His grace and mercy; from which it follows that God has again become our enemy on account of our crimes, though He may formerly have loved us for His Son's sake. St. Paul tells us that such reasoning is false, and that we should by no means give way to it, for he distinctly declares: "Christ died for us while we were yet sinners." Remember this, and be comforted by it. These words give us the explicit assurance, when our sins accuse us and threaten us with God's wrath and dire punishment, that Christ died for no other purpose than to save sinners, and for no other persons. If, therefore, we commit new sins, if our conscience accuses us, and if we have merited anew the vengeance of God, we ought ever to remember that Christ died for us as sinners,—for just such sinners as we are, and shall remain, though we may constantly exercise penitence and faith and new obedience with a good conscience. Yea, though we be ever so saintly, we will always need this consolation, that Christ died for us sinners, as St. Paul says: "Though I know of no sin, I am therefore not justified;" and the Psalmist, Psalm 143: "Enter not into judgment with Thy servant: for in Thy sight shall no man living be justified." It therefore remains a fixed fact, eternally unalterable, that the passion and death of Christ took place for our sin, no matter when committed, and while we were yet sinners, and that therefore we are freed from the eternal wrath of God, that we have forgiveness, that the atonement is made once for all, and that we can now obtain eternal life.

St. Paul continues: If God so loved us that He justified us through His blood, and if we earnestly believe that our sins are forgiven for His sake and that we are now pleasing in His sight, we ought to take comfort and rest assured that God will continue to be merciful unto us, and will save us in the end in heaven. He not only sacrificed Himself for us, but His life and victory are ours also.

The Apostle, when he spake these words, had in mind this severe tribulation, even of the pious, when they anxiously fear the wrath of God. He would fain give comfort by the assurance that God has averted His anger, and has employed mercy and grace toward us, even while we were yet sinners. If He did this then, how much less will He be wroth with us now after the redemption from sins by the death of His Son! This is surely a most effective sermon, preached against the unbelief which is so prone to nestle in our hearts. But Paul is not content with this assurance; he speaks of a still greater and more precious consolation to be derived from the death of Christ. He says: "For if, when we were enemies, we were reconciled to God by the death of His Son, much more, being reconciled, we shall be saved by His life." Would to God that we might have this comfortable assurance firmly rooted in our hearts. It is indeed an inexpressible deed of mercy that Christ died for sinners; for by His death we are redeemed. If now His death benefits us so much, should we not also enjoy blessings from His life? If He died in our behalf, and if His death is our gain, we can unhesitatingly rely upon it that His life now will also be of benefit unto us: He will keep us by His grace, and will defend us from the devil and the world, so that our faith may increase from day to day. Accordingly we see, to our edification and consolation, the Apostles directing our attention repeatedly to the joyous resurrection of our Lord Jesus. He who thus liveth after He died for us, will surely attend to our wants now, and will protect us in the true faith against all temptation. The Apostle would therefore encourage us in these words against all doubts and weakness of faith; he would tell us to put aside all terror of the wrath of God and of death, since our Father in heaven has so clearly commended His love toward us in giving His Son for us into death while we were yet sinners. If He did not spare this His most precious gift while we were yet in sin, He will surely bestow all blessings upon us now, since we have been cleansed from sin by the death of Christ.

Through Him and in His life we can have the power necessary to conquer death and hell; therefore we rejoice and trust in God, who loved us so exceedingly while we were yet sinners; yea, we know that for the sake of Christ, His Son, He will support us in our tribulations, and grant unto us in the end eternal life. Such a faith, and such confidence, is the Christian's true worship; we should therefore diligently seek it, pray for it, and retain it in our hearts. The Apostle Paul now concludes his exhortation to be of good cheer with these words: "We also joy in God through our Lord Jesus Christ, by whom we have now received the atonement."

He declares that we have received the atonement through Christ. We, on account of our sins, dared not hope for mercy from God. Now this is changed. Our sins are removed by the death of Christ, and we know that God no longer chides with us; He is our Friend, yea, our beloved Father. What then must be the result of such reconciliation? This, that we rejoice at such a merciful and loving God—a God who is the source of all love, whom we should praise, and upon whom our whole confidence in every need and sorrow should be placed. If we have God for a friend we need fear no injury; nothing can then terrify or harm us. An atonement has been made for sin; God is satisfied with us, and Christ our Mediator sits at the right hand of the Father. What matters it now if death does come and lay low our bodies, since we know that through Christ we shall rise again unto eternal life? Hence the Christians ought ever to rejoice, no matter what their fortunes in life may be; though pain may afflict their bodies, they can be glad in the spirit, and will praise their Father in heaven, upon whose love and mercy they depend, and under whose protection they are secure. Such a happy issue from ills we have through the atonement made by the death of Christ.

Hence we see what a horrible crime it is for the Pope and his adherents to disregard this atonement, and to direct the people to do good works and to depend upon human exertions and deeds in obtaining mercy of God and forgiveness of sins. Let us thank God from the very bottom of our hearts that we have been set free from this bondage of error, and that we can learn from so many testimonies of the Old and of the New Testament how to regard and apply the passion of Christ, so that we are enabled to say, whenever sin accuses: If we were no sinners, Christ need not have suffered for us, but since He did suffer, we will derive all consolation from His passion. Thus will we honor God and give thanks unto Christ our Lord. We can make no other return but to accept with heartfelt gratitude the precious gifts obtained by His passion and death.

If we do this, it must follow, as a necessary consequence, that we shun and hate sin, that amid various trials, by constant practice, we increase from day to day in faith, in love, in hope, and in patience. May God bless us in this endeavor, through Christ Jesus our Lord. Amen!

1

The Occurrences at the Mount of Olives

Then Jesus went with them to a place called Gethsemane, and he said to his disciples, "Sit here, while I go over there and pray." And taking with him Peter and the two sons of Zebedee, he began to be sorrowful and troubled. 38 Then he said to them, "My soul is very sorrowful, even to death; remain here, and watch with me." And going a little farther he fell on his face and prayed, saying, "My Father, if it be possible, let this cup pass from me; nevertheless, not as I will, but as you will." And he came to the disciples and found them sleeping. And he said to Peter, "So, could you not watch with me one hour? Watch and pray that you may not enter into temptation. The spirit indeed is willing, but the flesh is weak." Again, for the second time, he went away and prayed, "My Father, if this cannot pass unless I drink it, your will be done." And again he came and found them sleeping, for their eyes were heavy. So, leaving them again, he went away and prayed for the third time, saying the same words again. Then he came to the disciples and said to them, "Sleep and take your rest later on. See, the hour is at hand, and the Son of Man is betrayed into the hands of sinners. Rise, let us be going; see, my betrayer is at hand."

—MATTHEW 26:36-46

This is a beautiful narrative, and presents the true beginning of the sufferings of our Lord Jesus. It is profitable both for doctrine, showing how our Lord conducted Himself in His sufferings, and for consolation in the anguish of sin and an evil conscience.

The scholastics disputed much and diffusely about the events here narrated. It is, indeed, no trifling matter that such great fear, trembling and anguish should take possession of this person, who is, at the same time, eternal God and true man. But let men dispute about this as much as they will, and let them be ever so penetrating and subtile, it can never be fathomed! Yea, it is impossible to comprehend such grief and terror; they are beyond the reach of our minds, and this simply because the person who sustains them is exalted far above all things. We must, therefore, be content with understanding those inferior instances of sorrow or fear which we actually see. Such instances we have in the case of those poor wretches who are condemned to death for their crimes. Before these can become reconciled to their fate, they writhe in death's agony and struggle with death; and, sometimes, they cannot endure such anguish, and are even overwhelmed with fear, so that they can neither hear nor see, and do not understand what is spoken to them nor what they tell others, but are unconscious and even grow stiff, like one who knows neither where he is nor what ails him.

But here we must rather consider those whose grief and anguish are so intense, that they fear and tremble on their account; whose hearts are so pierced with wretchedness and terror that they would rather die than suffer them. Such excruciating pain is experienced by those hearts which wrestle with the fear of God's wrath or the violent onslaughts of despair. We may be assured that such great grief and terror assaulted our Lord on this occasion, so that He stood trembling and quaking before His disciples, who were affrighted and could not conceive what had befallen Him. This is beautifully indicated by Luke where he says that when the Lord "was come to His disciples, He found them sleeping for sorrow;" and here by the Lord Himself in the words: "My soul is exceeding sorrowful, even unto death," that is, I am so full of anguish, that I could die of agony. Our thoughts cannot go beyond this; for we know of no anguish that transcends such anguish unto death. But even the pangs of death cannot properly be compared with the agony of the Lord Jesus; for His was of such exceeding violence that no human heart could have borne it. And for this very reason it declares Christ to have been true man, else it could not have affected Him, and true God, else He could not have borne and conquered it. Our flesh and blood can not endure and conquer thus; human nature, yea, even the nature of angels, is by far too feeble to hold out in such distress. For it was not the only sorrow of the Lord Jesus that the hour was now at hand, in which He should be betrayed by Judas, taken captive by the Jews, nailed to the cross by the Gentiles, and suffer death; but that the sins of the whole world were upon Him, and that the death He was about to suffer was a death incurred by sin and the wrath of God. Since He became a substitute for us all, and took upon Himself our sins, that He might bear God's terrible wrath against sin and expiate our guilt, He necessarily felt the sin of the whole world, together with the entire wrath of God, and afterwards the agony of death on account of this sin. This is the point which makes it evident that we can neither adequately speak of such sufferings and anguish, nor even meditate upon them. While each of us has merely his own sins upon him, Christ alone bears the sins of all the world and must atone for them with His death. How very insignificant, therefore, the agony of all other men! The sins committed by the whole world, from the first man, Adam, to the judgment-day, are placed upon that one man who was born of the Virgin Mary, while our burden is so very trifling in comparison, and we still break down under it.

But what is this sorrow, anguish and trembling of the Lord to teach us? What benefit are we to derive from His fear and lamentation, and from His public confession that His heart is so filled with misery that He would rather not live? It was stated above that His being terrified at death should teach us that He is a true, natural man, possessing flesh and blood like ours, and that He is altogether of like mind with us, but without sin. For it is an innate quality of our human nature to shudder at the thought of death. But it is impossible that any other mortal should be moved with fear as great as that of the Lord Jesus, because upon Him rests the iniquity of all mankind, and because for this iniquity He must suffer the death which is merited by the sins of the whole human family. This, together with the fact that He really did bear this excessively great burden without succumbing or perishing under it, proves most forcibly that He is also God, and more than a man.

Therefore is this death-struggle a powerful weapon which we wield against the heretics, who teach that Christ was not true God and true man. For we are compelled to confess that both natures of Christ here show themselves mightily; that, while His sorrow and fear and His wrestling with death are a potent declaration of His true, natural humanity, His divine power is proclaimed by His submission to the will of God, and by

His conquering that agony which would have overpowered all men and all creatures.

But this conflict with death, besides being useful for doctrine and the strengthening of our faith, can be profitably employed by us in two other ways. Sin has so blinded and corrupted us poor mortals that we cannot sufficiently discern our own imperfections, else we would diligently guard against transgressions; for we perceive in ourselves and others that we regard sin as but a trifling injury, yea, more, that we delight in it. He who becomes enslaved to pernicious avarice does not hesitate to take twelve or fourteen per cent., and would think himself very prosperous if he could obtain a great amount of such usury. Just so it is with him whom Satan makes a slave to debauchery; such a one regards himself most fortunate when he can satisfy his sensual desire, and the gratification of his evil passions is his only ambition. This is the case too with other sins; we rejoice over our imagined success in committing them. All this misery originates in our not knowing what a dreadful calamity sin really is. If we could only comprehend the wrath of God which is revealed against sin, and His judgment which awaits it, we would no longer desire and love sin, but would fear it and flee from it as though it were sudden death.

This picture of our dear Lord's agony at the mount of Olives serves to furnish us with such knowledge and fear. For if we look carefully on this picture we shall behold an image of sin, at sight of which our hearts must recoil with horror. Only look earnestly at the person pictured here! He is the Son of God,—the everlasting Righteousness! And although He assumed our flesh and blood, His flesh and blood is altogether sinless. Yet, since He took upon Himself foreign sin, namely that of all the world, in order to atone for it, this sin of others so affected Him, filled Him with such grief and anguish, and so terrified Him, that He began to tremble and quake, confessing: "My soul is exceeding sorrowful, even unto death."

Now if the sins of others are able to inflict such agony upon this pious, innocent heart, what must not be the result if our own sins assail our naturally sinful and corrupt hearts, which are inclined to despair! God sometimes gives us instances of this result, that we may be influenced by terror; instances, in which sin rages in the soul to such a degree, that the poor miserable wretches destroy their own lives in order to be quickly released from such rackings of conscience. This is a certain sign that such sufferings of conscience are more grievous and intolerable than bodily death, notwithstanding that the latter is most violently opposed to our nature; for these wretched persons regard death as the means by which they can rid themselves of such sufferings. But it is a fatal means; for it is against that commandment of God which tells us, "thou shalt not kill." These people, therefore, only make themselves more worthy of God's wrath and of damnation. The proper means, by which we can with certainty get rid of this anguish, we shall consider hereafter.

Therefore, let us study this picture thoroughly, and not forget how our blessed Lord Jesus mourned and trembled at the mount of Olives. We should remember this especially when we are tempted by the devil, our own flesh and blood, or the wicked world, and when we perceive our great propensity to sin. Then let us reason thus: if sin is so mighty that it can affect Jesus Christ, my Lord and God, with the greatest grief, though it be not His own sin, but entirely that of others; how much more will it not tempt, grieve, terrify and oppress me, who am myself guilty of every sin to which I consented, and who can, at any rate, only with the greatest effort resist the fear of death and of the anger and judgment of God! Therefore, get thee hence, Satan, I will not follow thee! Thou makest it easy for me to sin, as though sin were a trifling matter; but in my Lord Jesus I perceive that it is the most intolerable burden, because it so agitated His innocent heart. Therefore this narrative is of great value to us as an admonition to live in the fear of God and to sin no more. And most certain is it, if we bear this picture in mind, and, in accordance with it, persevere in prayer against temptation, that God will mercifully assist us by His Holy Spirit, so that Satan must flee and our flesh be kept under restraint; while they who do not keep this picture in view are led and driven like haltered cattle whithersoever the devil will.

Especially does the prayer Christ offered here serve as such an admonition. These were His words: "O my Father, if it be possible, let this cup pass from me." Now it is evident that this was not possible; for it was necessary that He should offer up His body for the sins of the whole world, and die upon the cross. But what else is to be inferred from this, than that sin is such a great and terrible transgression that it was impossible for any creature to afford the least relief from its curse? But if we were to be delivered from this, it was necessary for the eternal Son of God to become man and to suffer death upon the cross for our sins; thus only could we become free from sin.

Therefore, again from this should we learn to know and judge sin correctly. If we desire to obey our own hearts and the devil, and to follow the example even of the world, it will be very easy for us to commit adultery and fornication, and to seek to profit by covetousness, by the practice of usury, and by extortion. We see this in the case of those who fall into such temptations that they can never get enough of sinning. O, do not serve your own heart, Satan and the world; let not the smooth fur deceive you, for it surely covers sharp, poisonous claws, and should these seize you it is all over with you, unless God succor you in an extraordinary way! For if sin could, in the manner we have related, assail and terrify Christ, who never was guilty of a single sin, what will become of you and me, whom sin has, at any rate, previously so corrupted that we can not do otherwise than fear, tremble and despair and fly from God, as did Adam and Eve in Paradise! Therefore, let us be on our guard, and not run wantonly into such danger. Let us ask God for His Holy Spirit, that He may assist us,—that we may by His help defend ourselves against sin. If we do this, we shall be indeed the better for the scene at the mount of Olives.

Let us proceed. Even as this scene has been employed by us as an admonition to fear God and to guard against sin, so does it serve, in the second place, for our consolation. No man is able so carefully to govern himself that his flesh and Satan will not succeed sometimes to mislead him with their clamor, so that he makes a mistake and falls into sin. And Satan incessantly prowls around the Christian for the special purpose of leading him into public offences, as we can see in the case of illustrious saints. How deeply David fell! And Peter the same! Now if this should happen to us also, and Satan should then come and harass our hearts by his representations of our sin, then we should again behold this picture of the mount of Olives, and turn our thoughts inward and say: O God, why is it that Jesus Christ, my Lord, Thy Son, trembles so? What is it that troubles Him? He prays that the cup might pass from Him. What is this cup? It is the bitter death upon the cross and nothing else. But why does He suffer this death, being without sin, holy and righteous? Alas, this is brought about by the sin of the world, which God has placed upon Him; this it is that oppresses and alarms Him!

But how must I apply this? what must I contemplate here? This will I consider here, and believe that it is true: if God has placed my sin upon Him, then am I most certainly released from sin; and because this is so, John the Baptist calls Him "The Lamb of God which taketh away the sin of the world." What accusation could I now bring against myself and my dear Lord Jesus? True, I am a sinner; I experience, alas! that my sins alarm me and that they always try to make me sad; I am afraid of God and His severe judgment. Nevertheless, of what could I accuse myself; and how could I censure my dear Lord Jesus? He trembles at the mount of Olives, and feels such anguish that His sweat is as it were great drops of blood; my sins, which He has taken upon Himself, and whose heavy burden He has borne, have brought Him to this. Therefore, I shall leave them there, and firmly hope that when I shall appear before God and His judgment, God shall find no sin in me. Not as though I were pious and had committed no sin, but that God Himself has taken away from me my iniquity and laid it on His Son. Isa. 53.

Thus the scene at the mount of Olives also serves for our consolation; it assures us that Christ has taken our sins upon Himself and rendered satisfaction for them. For how could we otherwise account for such fear and trembling? If our sins, therefore, rest upon Christ, we can be content; they are in the right place,—just where they belong. Upon us they do not lie well; for we and all men, yea and all creatures, are too weak to bear a single sin: it would crush us with its weight. Therefore, let them remain upon Christ, and see what happens Him on their account. He takes them to the cross with Him and even dies in consequence of them; but on the third day He appears as the Lord of sin, death and the devil; for they attacked Him with all their powers, but accomplished nothing. Now this should be our comfort, and we should thank God for the unspeakable grace, by which He removed from us the heavy burden which would have hurled us into the abyss of hell, and placed it upon His Son, Jesus Christ, our Lord, who, although He was sinless and God eternal, still toiled and drudged under it at the mount of Olives, until the bloody sweat flowed gently from Him. To this comfort let us cleave, and not permit sadness to oppress our hearts, but say: it is sufficient that my Lord Jesus mourned and trembled so; my lamentations can accomplish nothing. But if I make His agony my comfort, and on it base my hopes in life and death, then has He so labored for me with His griefs and fears that I must in future be joyful in Him and of good cheer, and not fear sin and death, but hope for God's grace and eternal life. Such exercise of faith and comfort in Christ is the true worship of God, pleasing unto Him; and since this exercise is the only means, by which we can worship God truly, poor, troubled consciences should make use of it whenever the burden of sin tortures and alarms the heart. Otherwise it is impossible to find any true, certain consolation in such misery.

But this history of the scene at the mount of Olives is also of use to us in teaching us, by Christ's example, how to conduct ourselves in times of fear, temptation and distress. The hour was now at hand when Judas should betray, the Jews capture, and the Gentiles crucify Christ. What does He do? He is "exceeding sorrowful" and full of fear. But this is not all. "He went a little further, and fell on His face, and prayed." We too must learn this; we dare not let trouble so affect us that we forget to pray. For it is also a necessary part of divine worship and pleasing to God, not to despair in anguish and distress, but, when these attack us, to lift up our hearts to Him, and seek His help. The 91. Psalm testifies to this, where God says: "He shall call upon me, and I will answer him; I will be with him in trouble; I will deliver him, and honor him." But this is very difficult for us; for we imagine, when God suffers anxiety and distress to come upon us, that He is angry with us and is our enemy; and, therefore, even if we do pray, we think that our prayers are vain and useless. But against this we can employ the comfort of Christ's agony, and thus drive back such thoughts. For if God were always angry when He suffers pains and distresses to come upon us, it would follow that He was angry with His dear Son. But the reverse is the case, as Solomon also says, namely, that the father scourgeth every son whom he receiveth, and whom the Lord loveth He chasteneth. Therefore, let no such thoughts deceive us; let us not regard God as an enemy because He permits us to suffer. We see here that He does not exempt His only begotten Son from suffering, but permits Him to feel sin and the agony of death, and to fear and tremble on their account. We should believe that God deals with us in the same way; that we are His children and that He desires to remain our Father, notwithstanding that He lets us suffer a little. For why would we be spared all those things, from which He did not exempt even His Only Begotten, whom He permitted to suffer that agony for us which we would have had to suffer forever in hell? Therefore, let us still follow Christ, and as we endure fear and distress with Him, even so let us learn to pray with Him, and doubt not that God will graciously hear our prayers!

And how did Christ pray? The prayer itself is a very useful and necessary pattern, which we should imitate, and never leave out of sight. He prays: "O my Father, if it be possible, let this cup pass from me; nevertheless, not as I will, but as Thou wilt." This petition He repeats three times, until finally, as Luke says, "there appeared an angel unto Him from heaven, strengthening Him."

Now this is the model prayer which we too should use in temptation and trouble. "O my Father," He prays, as though He would say: although my present anguish and alarm are so great that they make me exceeding sorrowful, even unto death, and that I see nothing before me but Thy terrible wrath, and death; still I do not doubt that Thou art my Father, that Thou dost love me, that Thou dost behold me and care for me. Therefore, I hope to be released from this agony. "If it be possible, let this cup pass from me;" that is, help me, and save me from these sufferings.

Even as Christ calls upon God, His Father, so must we also do. For, although He alone is the eternal Son of God, according to the 2. Psalm: "Thou art my Son; this day have I begotten Thee," yet we too are children and heirs of God by faith in Christ Jesus. We should, therefore, not merely utter these words in our prayers, but be fully confident that God, as our Father, desires our welfare, and will not forsake us, His children. For where such trust is wanting, there can be no sincere prayer, and there surely the thought is entertained that God is not our Father, that He does not want us, and that He is not concerned about us. But this is dishonoring God and robbing Him of His right name, "Father."

But let us learn still another lesson. Our dear Lord Jesus prays that His Father would let this cup pass from Him, and, as the true only begotten

Son, He expects everything good of His Father. Yet He adds these words: "Nevertheless, not as I will, but as Thou wilt." Let us do the same. Let us not on account of temptation and affliction think that God is angry with us; but turn to Him as the child turns to its father; for, because we believe in Christ, God will accept us as sons and as joint heirs with Christ; and let us call upon Him for help, saying: O blessed heavenly Father, see how hard it goes with me in this or that respect,—help, for the sake of Thy dear Son, Jesus Christ,—suffer me not to remain in this distress or to sink under it, and so on. With this God is well pleased. And it is His desire that we all, in every need, have such confidence in Him, in and through Christ; that we, firmly relying upon Him as our dear Father, call upon Him; and that we do not doubt at all that He, for Christ's sake, will not only be merciful to us as His dear children, but also heartily sympathize with us and therefore willingly help us. Still we must humble ourselves, and not insist upon having our will, but submit it to the will of God whether we shall still continue in misery; and, if this is His will, show our obedience by patiently bearing such a delay of deliverance, as we can see that Christ here did.

But the question might here occur to us: why does Christ here pray thus, while in His prayer in the 17. chap. of John He does not use a single word which implies that He commits the decision, whether He shall obtain His request or not, to the will of God? There He says: "Father, the hour is come; glorify Thy Son. O Father, glorify Thou me. Keep through Thine own name those whom Thou hast given me. I pray that Thou shouldest keep them from the evil. Sanctify them through Thy truth." Also: "Father, I will that they also, whom Thou hast given me, be with me where I am," &c. This entire prayer shows that He will have His request granted and not denied. But why does He not pray in the same way here? Answer: the want, for which the Lord prays here, is a temporal, bodily want. Now we must, in all things pertaining to this bodily life, submit our will to that of God; for, as Paul says, "we know not what we should pray for." It is, besides, often necessary for us that God should leave us under the cross and in distress. Since God alone knows what is good for us, we should prefer His will and renounce our own, rendering obedience with patience.

When, however, bodily affairs are not the subject of our prayer, but eternal blessings, God's will is manifest and unalterable; it is His will that all men should be saved, that they should acknowledge their sin and believe in its forgiveness through Christ. Such eternal blessings we receive when God pardons our iniquity, upholds us by His Word, sanctifies us, and gives us the Holy Spirit and everlasting life; and such blessings as these it is that Christ implores for the Christian Church in John 17. Therefore, when praying for such heavenly, eternal gifts, it is not necessary to commit it to God's will, whether He will hear us or not. We should know that He will give us these things willingly and most certainly; for we have His Word which declares to us His will in this respect. "God so loved the world," Christ tells us, "that He gave His only begotten Son, that whosoever believeth in Him should not perish, but have everlasting life." Behold, here we have God's will with reference to our salvation. Boldly, therefore, let us pray in accordance with this will, just as Christ, John 17., prays: "Father, I will that they be where I am!" Be this also our prayer: Father, I pray and I will have it so, that Thou forgive my sins for the sake of Thy Son, Jesus Christ, who has expiated their guilt, having made an atonement for them by His death!

In this way, however, we cannot perceive God's will in regard to bodily temptation and distress. We do not know whether it would contribute to our salvation and to the honor of God, if He should, according to our desire, quickly release us from sickness, poverty or other troubles. We should, therefore, pray for help indeed; but submit it to the will of God whether we shall be helped soon or shall continue in our affliction. And should God not relieve us immediately, and in the manner we wish, our prayer shall still not be useless, but God shall strengthen our hearts and impart to us grace and patience, so that we can bear our affliction and triumph in the end. The example here of Christ proves this; God, His Father, would not let the cup pass from Him; still He sent Him an angel who strengthened Him. So it shall be with us too, even if God should delay or refuse His help. But in regard to spiritual wants we are certain of being heard: God will, for Christ's sake, cheerfully forgive our sins and save our souls; therefore, we can pray for this with sure confidence, and it were a sin to doubt it.

This is the third lesson, about prayer in temptation. But we are very slow at learning it, as the example before us of the disciples plainly shows.

Temptation was in store for them too, and, therefore, the Lord admonishes them to pray, so that they might not enter into temptation. For in such a case prayer is the only and the best preventive and remedy. But the flesh is so weak and sluggish, that when the danger is greatest and prayers are most needed we slumber and sleep; that is, anguish overtakes us and molests us so severely, that we think all opposition is vain and useless. Temptation or the fall is the result of this, as it was in the case of the disciples. But our gracious and compassionate God, who has promised us assistance and mercy through His Son Jesus Christ, pardons this weakness and rescues us from temptation, if we heed His admonition, again to seek consolation and help with Him.

This, then, is the history of the agony at the mount of Olives, which should be diligently considered and properly applied. This is done when we, in the first place, learn from it how very heavy a burden sin must be, since it so oppressed and tortured the Son of God that He trembled, and that great drops of blood fell from Him to the ground, and when we, therefore, look well to ourselves and flee from sin.

This is done when we, secondly, draw consolation from this history in those times of distress and temptation which cannot fail to come upon us too; we see how the Son of God bore our sins.

We make the right use of this history when we, in the third place, continue instant in prayer, in every temptation, according to Christ's command: "Watch and pray, that ye enter not into temptation."

He who thus employs the occurrences at the mount of Olives, shall remain in the fear of God and in true faith, and shall find comfort and deliverance in all manner of dangers and temptations. May our blessed Lord Jesus grant this to us all through His Holy Spirit. Amen.

2

The Seizure of Christ in the Garden

> While he was still speaking, Judas, one of the Twelve, arrived. With him was a large crowd armed with swords and clubs, sent from the chief priests and the elders of the people. Now the betrayer had arranged a signal with them: "The one I kiss is the man; arrest him." Going at once to Jesus, Judas said, "Greetings, Rabbi!" and kissed him. Jesus replied, "Do what you came for, friend." Then the men stepped forward, seized Jesus and arrested him.
>
> —MATTHEW 26:47–50

This is the second part of the history of the events which took place in the garden. Here we are told, in the first place, how Judas, one of the twelve, after he had conferred with the Jews on the subject, and sold the Lord Jesus for thirty pieces of silver, (each of which, according to our coin, is worth about half of a florin), finally also betrayed Him in the garden.

This was a very wicked and scandalous deed, and it is, even at this day, so offensive to many wise and sensible people that, on account of it, they speak evil of the Gospel, and consider its doctrine injurious. For, since Satan keeps no holiday, but chiefly sows his tares among the wheat where he sees the good seed coming forth hopefully, it is no wonder that among those who possess God's pure Word there are found so many disciples of Judas, that is, knaves and infidels.

When the world sees such deeds it quickly passes judgment upon them. Thus we are often compelled to hear how our adversaries of the present day lay all the blame for such offences upon the doctrine, and say: If the doctrine were correct it would also produce good fruit, but since there are so many more offences in the world now than there were formerly, it must follow that the doctrine is false.

True, the Insurrection of the Peasants, in the year 1525, occurred after the Gospel had been brought to light. Then followed the Sacramentarians, Anabaptists, and other sects, the like of which no one heard nor saw before the Gospel came to us. But does it, therefore, follow that the doctrine is bad, and that such offences were produced by the doctrine? We shall find the answer to this if we examine that villain, Judas, who was neither Gentile nor Turk; neither was he a Jew of that kind which offered resistance to Christ and paid no attention to the Word of God. Matthew says that he was "one of the twelve," whom Christ had called to preach, to baptize in His name, to cast out devils, and to perform all manner of glorious miracles. And since the Lord knew his knavery from the beginning, there is no doubt that He instructed Judas more than the rest, always admonishing him not to give place to sin and temptation. In connection with the Holy Supper the Evangelists specially mention that the Lord would every now and then let fly a word or two at him, if, peradventure, he might be turned from his sin. And, finally, He gave him a sop, no doubt casting upon him a longing look, as though He would say: O, thou poor fellow, how canst thou be my enemy? What cause do I give thee for intending such things against me?

But since nothing could prevail with him, and since he gave place to temptation and even yielded to it, the Lord said unto him: "That thou doest, do quickly;" as if He wanted to say: I see well enough that all warnings and admonitions are in vain; go, then; there is no help for thee.

Now what shall we say to this, that the desperate villain commits such a hideous sin, and harbors such malice and bitterness against his Lord and Master, in whose name he also had performed miracles, that, for the sake of a trifling sum of money, he betrays and sells the innocent, pious, gracious and gentle Lord and Saviour, well knowing that it would cost His life? Whom shall we blame for this? Here we read that he was one of the twelve. Shall we, therefore, say that the Lord Jesus and the doctrine which Judas heard of Christ are to blame? If Christ had taught him better things, would he have done them? But supposing that this thought did occur to you, would you not shudder at it, and fear so to accuse the Lord Jesus? For you know that He is holy and righteous, and the enemy of every vice; yea, that the object of all His teaching and preaching was to check and ward off sin and save from death. Why, then, would you impute such crime to our dear Lord? You should rather say: If Judas had not been such a scandalous, wicked villain that every friendly warning was thrown away upon him, and could not free him from his malice, he would have behaved himself differently; for, although the other Apostles were so very weak that they were offended because of the Lord Jesus, they still do not fall into sin so monstrous as that of Judas, who must, therefore, have been such an arrant knave that nothing could save him.

Why then do you not pass the same judgment upon similar cases which occur at present? Why do you blame and blaspheme the Holy Gospel for that which wicked men and Satan have committed? For if Christ Himself cannot preach with such earnestness and power that Judas ceases to be a scoundrel, as he was from the beginning, it is no wonder that the like is seen among us also, and that not all obey the Word.

The Peasants' War, as stated before, followed after God had restored the Gospel to us; we have no desire to deny this. But must the Gospel, therefore, be reproached for this offence and mischief? Were there not insurrections and offences in the world before the Gospel was preached? We should rather argue as follows: Satan hates the Gospel; men are by nature corrupt and inclined to evil; therefore, Satan and the evil world have caused these offences, so that the good seed, which is the pure, wholesome doctrine, might be despised by men.

Thus originated the Sacramentarians and Anabaptists also, of whom no one heard before the coming of the Gospel. But the Gospel is not to blame. The devil, and then the temerity of idle and frivolous hearts which do not hold fast the Word, but follow their own wisdom, whistled for this jig, and prepared this terrible evil and such pernicious scandal.

Even at this day, as we see, this scandal prevails, that avarice and usury, lasciviousness and gluttony, and other vices are more common among those who boast of the Gospel than they were formerly under the papacy. Whence comes this filth? Is it learned from the Gospel? Are the preachers to blame? No, such thoughts be far from us! That would be abusing and calumniating God and His dear Word, and the Gospel ministry which is God's most precious gift. But we must blame the very devil, who is chagrined when he sees the field well prepared and sowed with good seed;

for this admirably impairs his kingdom. Therefore, while the house-holder sleeps, he comes with his seed of wickedness, and scatters tares over the whole field.

But thus he does not bring it about that the tares alone grow. For even as Judas, one of the twelve, was a rascal, while the other disciples, notwithstanding their frailty, did not fall into such shocking sin; so, while many and very common offences exist, we also find many noble, pious Christians, who abide in the Word in all sincerity, live in the fear of God and guard against offences. We should be satisfied with this and thank God for it. And since we cannot get rid of this Judas, we shall have to tolerate him, still remembering that not all are like him, but that some of the disciples turned out better.

The instance of the spoiled child, Judas, teaches us, first, that we must not revile the Gospel like the Papists, but recognize the true cause of offences in the devil and in those disobedient hearts which believe not the Word and will not be bettered by the Word.

Secondly, it teaches us, by that dreadful fall, to fear God. For, as was said above, Judas was no common person, but an Apostle, and, doubtless, possessed many noble, excellent gifts; this is indicated by his having a special office among the disciples, the Lord having appointed him house-holder, or steward.

Now this Judas, who was an Apostle, who in Jesus' name preached repentance and remission of sins, who baptized, cast out devils, and did other miracles, apostatized most shamefully from God and became the enemy of Christ, whom, for a little silver, he sold, betrayed and delivered over to be slaughtered. And since such a terrible misfortune befell so great a man as Judas, we surely have reason never to feel secure, but to fear God, to beware of sin, and, without ceasing, to pray that God would not lead us into temptation, but that when temptation comes upon us He would mercifully sustain us, deliver us from it, and not suffer us to stick fast in it. For unless the greatest caution is exercised and the weapon of prayer is diligently used, it is a very easy matter to fall and commit sin.

The case of Judas stands thus. He was an avaricious fellow; the Evangelists mention several times that he was in the habit of stealing from the treasury, which, according to the Lord's appointment, was in his care.

He gave the reins to this sin and became addicted to it. He permitted men to talk and to preach to him, as, alas! some of the miserable, provoking Christians of our day let themselves be talked and preached to; but went nevertheless and stole wherever he could, and thought himself in no danger because he was an Apostle as well as the rest.

Because he thus gave place to sin, his carnal security finally brought him so far that the devil entered into him quite, and urged him on to the attainment of his outrageous purpose of betraying his dear Lord and Master for fifteen florins. Since the devil was thus successful in leading Judas to this act of treachery, the greater wretchedness followed that Judas fell into despair and hanged himself on account of such sin. This is the end the devil had in view.

Now we should diligently observe this case of Judas and, as already stated, be admonished by it to keep a clear conscience; to live in the true fear of God; and not to cease praying that God would uphold us by His Word, rule us by His Holy Spirit, and keep us from sin. For if we make a mistake in an apparently trifling matter even, unspeakably great misery may ensue. Our dear Lord Jesus, in the 11. chapter of Luke, warns us against this, saying: "When the unclean spirit is gone out of a man, he walketh through dry places, seeking rest; and finding none he saith, I will return unto my house whence I came out. And when he cometh, he findeth it swept and garnished. Then goeth he, and taketh to him seven other spirits more wicked than himself; and they enter in and dwell there; and the last state of that man is worse than the first." We have instances of this before us. Before the blessed Gospel came to light again, the devil enjoyed perfect tranquility; he had ensnared nearly every heart by a spurious worship and by reliance on good works. But God has now banished him by the Gospel, that we might know that God is not served and that we are not benefited by the celebration of masses, by vigils, pilgrimages and monkery. God's Word has taught us a different form of worship, which the 2. Ps. calls "kissing the Son;" and God from heaven declared it "hearing and believing in His Son." This we know.

Let us see what takes place now. The devil would gladly come back to his old home; but he can not, for he finds the entrance blocked up and himself exposed by the light of God's Word. "Then goeth he and taketh to him seven," that is, innumerable, "other spirits more wicked than himself; and they enter in and dwell there." We see that most men are under the impression that they can lead a lewd life, practice covetousness und usury, lie and deceive, and still be in no danger, and be good Christians all the while. Wherever there is a hole left open for the devil, even if we would think it too small for him to peep through, it is large enough for him to stick his head in and drag his whole body after. In this way he entered into Judas too. We might think his stealing ten or twenty dollars a very little matter; but because he continually hankered after the pleasures of this sin, and did not suffer God's Word to restrain him, the devil finally prevails on him, for the sake of money, to lead his blessed Lord and Master like an ox to the slaughter.

Hence the warning: Fear God and shun sin. But if you will continue in sin, you may look out for the danger, to which you thus expose yourself; for the devil does not go to work with the intention of conferring favors on you. He prompted Judas to avarice until he led him through despair to the gallows. Let this be your warning, and desist in time! Earnestly beseech God that He would, for Christ's sake, not impute to you your iniquity, and then reform! This is the will of God. He permitted this dreadful example of Judas to be given that we might study it and recoil from it. For who would have thought that such a terrible sin could have such an insignificant beginning! O, do not make light of this; do not think in your heart: I can do so and so, and still be a Christian,—I will make amends some day, &c. The devil is too cunning for you; when he has once spun his web about you, it will not be easy for you to tear yourself away.

So much for the example of Judas. From another point of view our text furnishes us comfort and admonition. It is always the case, that, as our Lord Jesus fared on earth, so must His Church and precious Gospel fare to the end of the world. Judas, one of His disciples, betrays Christ. Thus, they who hold churchly offices and bear ecclesiastical titles and names, wish to be regarded as the heads and rulers of the Church; it is not thirty pieces of silver, as in the case of Judas, but many thousand dollars that make them traitors and archenemies of the Church. See the Pope, for instance; he has the very bag of Judas hanging from his neck, and is so fond of money and possessions that he takes them in exchange for the Gospel, which he betrays and sells, and with which he deals as the Jews dealt with the Lord Jesus before Caiphas and Pilate! And just as Judas attaches to himself the servants of the high priests and rulers, so the Pope gathers about him monks, priests, schools, bishops, and his entire brood of spiritless Sodomites, who help him capture Christ, that is, persecute and denounce the Gospel, as if it were the most hellish heresy. And finally Pilate, the civil government, also joins them, and attempts to exterminate the Gospel with the sword.

This has been taking place a long time, ever since the Pope received such great power and authority. And even to-day the ranks of Judas' army are being swelled by those who use the Gospel for coining gold, with which they then feed their avarice, ambition, pride and lust. These should, indeed, consider Judas' end. For it has been resolved that neither the Pope nor any other traitors of Christ and His Word, let them be ever so exalted and wise, shall be blessed in the possession of that price of blood obtained by selling Christ or His Gospel. Sooner or later remorse shall come; and, should no amendment follow, these Gospel-venders, together with Judas their master, shall receive eternal death and damnation as their recompense, in the depths of hell. Let no one doubt this! Were it not for the denunciation of such a terrible doom, we should have reason for being indignant on account of these miserable fellows, Pope, cardinals, bishops, priests and monks, they fare so sumptuously every day. But, my friends, let us not envy these fattening hogs because God permits them for a little while to wallow in the filth of their obscene lusts; the thirty pieces of silver, for which they sell their Lord every day, will lie heavily enough upon their souls when Christ shall say to them: "Depart from me, ye cursed, into everlasting fire, prepared for the devil and his angels." Besides, their heart and conscience cannot be long satisfied. For, although they may for a time live in thoughtlessness, security and riot, when eventually that little black dog, Remorse by name, begins to bark, it will go badly enough with them; then, with eternal ruin yawning before them, they shall see and feel what Isaiah meant in his 48. chapter, when he said: "There is no peace unto the wicked." We have instances before us at the present time of the terrible end which came upon several of the most prominent adversaries of the Gospel.

This we say with reference to Judas, of whom the Evangelists tell us how he sold Christ, led the Jews into the garden and betrayed the Lord

Jesus with a kiss, which, according to Matthew, was the sign he should give the Jews. This is also applicable to those false prophets who, because they have the authority of office, mislead poor consciences with false and impure doctrine.

The Evangelist John mentions two remarkable miracles performed in the garden by our Lord Jesus. One of them is the following. When the Jews had come into the garden to the Lord Jesus, He asked them, "Whom seek ye?" And when they had answered Him, "Jesus of Nazareth," His reply, "I am He," so frightened them that they all went backward and fell to the ground as if they had been struck by lightning. This was done by a special and divine power, which the Lord showed forth at that time, not alone to terrify the Jews, but also to strengthen His disciples. These, instead of venturing, as they did, to rescue Jesus by force, might have concluded from this display of power that if the Lord did not choose to give Himself up unto death, He was able to defend Himself and resist His enemies without calling upon others for assistance or protection. The Lord wanted no violence done, and severely remonstrates with Peter on this subject, as we shall see. This miracle, therefore, serves as a protection against that gulf of offences, in which both the Jews and afterwards even the disciples came near drowning. Since the Lord suffered Himself to be seized, allowed the Jews to play on Him their wanton pranks, and finally permitted Himself to be so shamefully executed upon the cross, even the disciples were so offended that they forgot all those miracles which they had seen Him do and all those powerful sermons they had heard of Him, and thought that everything was over with Him now,—that their hopes had been all in vain. And, on the other hand, the unbelieving and malicious Jews felt certain that their object would be well accomplished as soon as they should have Him nailed to the cross.

How glorious, therefore, this miracle! The great multitude of Jews, armed with swords and staves, provided with authority from the rulers, and eager and desperate to do its work, is driven back and so frightened that they all fall to the ground as if some enemy had violently thrust them down; and all this by the single word, "I am He," spoken by a man who stood alone and weaponless, and who did nothing more than speak most friendly words. The disciples see this great miracle; the Jews also feel its force; still it is soon forgotten. Yea, because Christ so patiently submitted to His sufferings and used no other power against His enemies, they took Him to be a mere man.

But they should in all reason have argued as follows: If this Man is able, with a single word, which is neither invective nor curse, but only a gentle reply, as with a thunderbolt, to strike down such great, strong, bold and armed men, then must there surely be a deep meaning in His voluntary resignation. He is able to defend and protect Himself, but instead of doing so He submits. He therefore does not desire the aid of men. And, although He now hides His power and permits the Jews to do with Him what they will, this shall, by no means, be the end of it. Dismay must seize His enemies, but He must conquer. For that divine power which He showed forth so frequently, and which He manifests here in the garden especially by the single word, "I am He," cannot remain withheld and repressed for a great length of time, &c.

The disciples in particular should have regarded the miracle in this light. There can be no doubt that it was to this end that the Lord here revealed His divine might. But alas! the effects of this were too quickly lost upon both parties. The Jews, intent on their mischief, feared no further. The disciples, running hither and thither, now sad, now terrified, had no hope of ever again seeing their Lord and Master, to say nothing of their despairing of ever being further benefited by Him. This was the "hour of darkness," as Christ calls it in the Gospel according to St. John, in which offences prevailed and the devil exercised His power. It was for this reason that the Lord so earnestly admonished the disciples, "Watch ye and pray, lest ye enter into temptation."

The other miracle is similar to this. It is performed by Christ's second answer: "I have told you that I am He; if therefore ye seek me, let these go their way." Our dear Lord is alone, and has neither sword nor spear; whereas Judas, the traitor, comes upon Him with a great multitude. We would think that our dear Lord had reason to entreat and beg, seeing that He stands against such numbers. But He advances and commands the Jews that they should let His disciples alone, and not lay hands on one of them. This is a stern command: *Sinite hos abire*, "Let these go;" and we see that it was not given in vain. For they, no doubt, set out with the thought that they would capture the whole company, Master and disciples. But this command compels them to desist from their intention of taking the disciples, although Peter did not deserve this, because he lay about him with his sword.

But why does the Lord give such a command? It is not incorrect to say, that He wishes to show by this that He esteems His own life more lightly than the lives of His disciples; for He rescues them while He lets Himself be taken and bound. For the same reason He calls Himself a "Good Shepherd" who "giveth His life for the sheep;" and shows us His love as a special example, saying: "Greater love hath no man than this, that a man lay down his life for his friends. Ye are my friends, if ye do whatsoever I command you." We clearly see that He is silent about His own person; the Jews do with Him what they please and He does not hinder them. But He wants them to let His disciples alone and to do no violence to them. This shows that He cares more for them than for Himself.

This was not done without a purpose. Our dear Lord Jesus wanted no partners in the sufferings before Him. For, as the 53. chapter of Isaiah tells us, "The Lord hath laid on Him," on Him alone, "the iniquity of us all," and this He had to bear alone and for this offer Himself as a sacrifice. True, the disciples also were afterwards compelled to suffer for the sake of Christ and His Word, as Christ had told James and John: "Ye shall indeed drink of the cup that I drink of."

But the suffering of the Lord Jesus was a suffering for my sins, for thy sins, and for the sins of all the world; so that now, for Christ's sake, God will not only forgive and pass by these sins, but also bestow righteousness and eternal life upon me, upon thee, and upon all believers. For this reason Christ desired to be alone, and permitted no one to be seized nor to suffer with Him.

This should be preached in all churches throughout Christendom, and with all diligence should the people be continually taught to hope for the forgiveness of every sin, alone through the sufferings and death of Christ, &c. But this is not done by the abominable Pope and his scandalous scribblers and shriekers. Their tongues, indeed, confess that Jesus is the Lamb of God, which taketh away the sin of the world; but their actions give their words the lie. This they prove by their so woefully deceiving the poor people with their falsehoods; telling them to invoke deceased saints, of these saints to seek pardon for their sins, and with the merits of these saints to console themselves, and in virtue of their doing this they receive indulgences. This is as much as saying that Christ desired associates in His sufferings, and accomplished nothing by Himself.

That the Lord was afterwards crucified between "two thieves" has its peculiar signification, viz., to show for whom Christ's sufferings avail, and upon whom they are lost; of which, however, we have no time to speak at present. But here in the garden the word is: *Sinite hos abire*, "Let these go;" I alone am fit for this work; to suffer and to die for the sins of the world is an office which belongs to me alone. Neither John, Peter or James can do anything in this; let all these go their way! I, "I am He;" me you must lay hold on, me capture, me bind, me crucify, unto me it is given to take away the sin of the world; and all who believe in me, that is, comfort themselves with my suffering and death, shall find a gracious God and eternal life.

This, then, is the second part of the history of those things concerning Christ which occurred in the garden. It teaches us: first, to bear in mind this terrible fall of the Apostle Judas, to abide in the fear of God, to avoid sin, and to be diligent in prayer that God may in mercy prevent us from falling as Judas fell; secondly, that we also, as true Christians, shall be sorely molested by the avarice of some Judas or other, that we must patiently endure this and cling to the consolation that Christ, though He may be weak in us now, will show His power at the proper time, and graciously protect and preserve us. The Ever-living Father of our Lord and Saviour Jesus Christ grant us this by His Holy Spirit. Amen.

3

Christ Refusing to be Rescued by Peter's Sword

With that, one of Jesus' companions reached for his sword, drew it out and struck the servant of the high priest, cutting off his ear. "Put your sword back in its place," Jesus said to him, "for all who draw the sword will die by the sword. Do you think I cannot call on my Father, and he will at once put at my disposal more than twelve legions of angels? But how then would the Scriptures be fulfilled that say it must happen in this way?" In that hour Jesus said to the crowd, "Am I leading a rebellion, that you have come out with swords and clubs to capture me? Every day I sat in the temple courts teaching, and you did not arrest me. But this has all taken place that the writings of the prophets might be fulfilled." Then all the disciples deserted him and fled.

—MATTHEW 26:51–56.

This is the third and last part of the scene in the garden, or at the mount of Olives. It relates how Peter drew his sword, intending to rescue his Master by force, after they had taken the Lord Jesus.

The facts here narrated, in the first place, teach us a necessary and useful lesson concerning the sword, or temporal power, showing who shall and who shall not wield it, and what punishment is due to him who presumes to bear it without a call. Secondly, whereas Peter in this case makes use of the sword to liberate Christ, and still Christ forbids his doing so, it becomes necessary here to treat the question, whether we dare or should defend the Gospel with the sword, so that the civil government may be properly instructed in both respects, and neither act contrary to its office, nor do more than its calling demands. Otherwise both Church and State would be unjustly dealt by, which injustice would be most certainly punished.

Now as far as Peter is concerned, it is manifest that he was a minister or ecclesiastic, whom it does not behoove to bear the sword, according to the words of Christ: "The princes of the Gentiles exercise dominion. But it shall not be so among you." Therefore, Peter does wrong in resorting to the sword for the Lord's protection, and Christ rebukes him for it. This was not a matter that could be decided with the sword, for Christ says: Even if our cause did depend upon our defence, "Thinkest thou that I cannot now pray to my Father, and He shall presently give me more than twelve legions of angels?" This was as much as saying: It is now expedient for me to suffer; I will not have any one to draw his sword on my account and strike for my protection. But Christ administers this rebuke to Peter for the reason, also, that to him as a private person the sword did not belong. Therefore, He not only commands Peter to put up his sword, but also pronounces the terrible threat: "All they that take the sword shall perish with the sword."

We must duly heed these words; for by them the Lord makes a distinction among men, informing us that some wield the sword by divine commission. These are all they who, by the proper and ordinary means, are called to the temporal government for the purpose of ruling, of guarding and promoting the public weal, and of preventing public offences. Into the hands of these God gives the sword, that is, it is God's will and institution that they bear the sword, not for their own emolument, but for the good of their subjects, as St. Paul says: A ruler "is the minister of God, a revenger to execute wrath upon him that doeth evil." For since words will not persuade the world, severity must be used, and people must be compelled to desist from crime, so that the common peace and unity may be maintained and a restraint be put upon wantonness. If the thief persist in stealing, let him dangle from the gallows, and then we shall be secure from him. Let the wanton villain who takes delight in injuring every one, and who strikes and stabs for the sake of a mere word, find justice on the gibbet, and then he will let people alone; he will henceforth strike and stab no more, for the hangman puts an excellent stop to such work. Therefore, the civil government serves God by using the sword against sin and scandal; for God, who will not leave offences and sin unpunished, has given the command to do this. God makes this distinction among men, that to a few He intrusts the sword, with it to ward off mischief and to protect the subjects.

But the rest, who have not received such authority, must, by no means, handle the sword, and never draw it except at the command of the temporal government. But should they take it on their own responsibility, the judgment written here will most certainly not fail: "All they that take the sword shall perish with the sword." In every history we see how they who took revenge into their own hands never succeeded well with it; all rebels had to suffer finally and perished with the sword. All manslayers who wickedly murdered others were either delivered to the executioner or perished in some other way, or else went so astray in the miserable life they led that they would a thousand times better have died. Such is the regulation of God He will have it so, that all they that take the sword, and do not wait until God or the government gives it to them, shall perish with the sword; this cannot be changed. Let every one, therefore, be careful and bridle his wrath; let him either patiently bear his wrongs and subdue his passion, or else seek justice in the proper and divinely sanctioned way. What this is, has been sufficiently pointed out. Since God has given temporal governments the command to restrain offences and defend the pious with the sword, we must seek safety at the hands of these governments and inform against the offender. We must do this not alone for our security, but also to the end that offences be resisted, that malice be hindered, and that they who exercise temporal authority may properly discharge the duties of their office. For neither a mayor of a town nor a ruler of a land can be acquainted with every disturbance, and still their office makes them responsible to God for the quelling of all offences and uproars. Now if you and every body else would choose to keep silent about your wrongs, this would only increase the mischief and be giving the occasion for your own hurt, both of which results would be wrong, and both of which you can prevent by calling upon the government for protection. Should the government, however, upon your petition do nothing in this matter, and not help you to your rights, then observe this: Bear your wrongs patiently and beware of revenging yourself, lest your righteous cause become unrighteous before God and man.

But what then becomes of the words of Christ: "Whosoever shall smite thee on thy right cheek, turn to him the other also. And if any man will sue thee at the law, and take away thy coat, let him have thy cloak also," &c.? We answer: Both of these commands were given that we might be restrained from taking revenge into our own hands, and that we might rather suffer all things, and wait for the judgment of the Heavenly Judge, who is not so slow and heedless in conducting His office, as the civil authorities frequently are in conducting theirs. Christ here does not forbid our complaining to the government of the injury that is done us; He does not impose silence upon us.

But, you ask, do I not seek revenge when I make complaint against him who has harmed me? Most certainly; but you do right by this, provided you do it in the proper way and without anger or hatred towards your neighbor. For this is not your own revenge, but the revenge instituted by God for the purpose of checking scandal and protecting every one in the possession of his own. In short, he who has not been commanded to use the sword and still arrogates it to himself, to revenge himself or others, subjects himself to the judgment and condemnation of God: "All they that take the sword shall perish with the sword." Whenever, therefore, you or yours are injured, beware of the improper course of grasping the sword yourself and being your own defender! But make use of the correct means, that is, bring the matter before your government and let this protect and succor you; God commanded it to do this and ordained it for this. If you do this you do well, and will be safe against meddling with the affairs of others. But if the government either will not or can not help you, then endure your afflictions, touch not the sword, and let God be your Avenger; He surely will avenge you and also punish the government for its negligence!

But should a cut-throat come upon me in the forest, or a ruffian attack me on the highway, with the intention to harm me, and I had no time to seek the protection of the government, must I suffer myself to be injured or murdered? No; for in such a case the government permits every one to defend his person and his life against violence and outrage; for whenever she can lay hold on these villains, she executes them without delay. For this and other reasons Moses, according to the command of God, prescribed the appointment of several cities of refuge, to which the manslayer might resort who had taken life not intentionally, nor for revenge, nor in wrath, but accidentally or in pressing necessity. The civil authorities also follow this rule and recognize the lawfulness of self-defence. But in all other cases remember that "All they that take the sword shall perish with the sword."

But as they who, having no right to the sword, still continue to usurp the power of the sword, do not seek lawful vengeance and wish to administer vengeance themselves; even so, on the other hand, they, to whom God has given the sword that they might diligently wield it, are always inclined to be too mild, as though God had given a fox's tail into their hand instead of a keen-edged sword. These latter also commit great sin and are grievously disobedient before God, and they also shall be very sorely punished for their conduct. For where the civil government does not oppose public scandal with reasonable severity, there God Himself must eventually interfere as Judge and use the sword. And at the advent of this Judge, not only an individual or two, but an entire city or land must suffer for these sins. This we learn from many passages of Scripture and from numerous instances before us. It is, therefore, necessary that magistrates do not become lazy or indulgent, but that they exercise a becoming earnestness and a vigilant supervision, and that they apply punishment wherever offences exist; thus they satisfy the demands of their office and please God. But, as we have already said, this is an unpleasant duty; men take no delight in it, as can be shown by examples. For how often do we not find mildness used where it should not be used, and the most heinous offences lightly punished! How frequently are not hindrances interposed, and intercession made, so that crimes escape unpunished!

But should we not have more regard for the divine command than for human intercession? God says: Receive from my hand this sword; I give it thee that thou shalt, in my stead, punish every one under thy control who is guilty of public offence, no matter whether he be friend or foe, exalted or low, rich or poor, noble or ignoble; let the sword descend wherever there are offences, so that these may not prevail! This is what God says to every government. But, on the other hand, men come with their petitions, asking that this or that one might be pardoned, or punished mildly, although the most terrible trespasses, *atrocia delicta*, have been committed, such as brutal murder, incest, and the like, &c. And it often happens that man's intercession has more influence upon the government than the stringent command of God. I leave it to you to judge whether this is right, and what must be the result under God's justice.

Sometimes offences are public, but the civil government refuses to punish them unless some one volunteers as plaintiff. Because no one brings complaint, it lets the matter pass. This is downright heedlessness, both in regard to God's command and to the office. The watchman is stationed on the tower, by day and by night to be on the lookout for fires or other mischief that may occur within or without the city, and then to publish the danger in time, and to warn against losses. In like manner God has placed the temporal ruler far above all other people, that he might exercise watchfulness, and when he sees offences about to be committed, be they great or small, to put them down with the sword before they become formidable, no matter whether any one has complained or not. Therefore, "he beareth the sword," as Paul says, to be "a terror to evil works," so that peace may be enjoyed by all and wantonness may be resisted. And the Lord commands here that the sword shall not rest nor be idle, but destroy those who take it. Thus we see that both parties fail to do their duty: they who have not the sword, wish to have it and lay about them with it, like Peter here; but they who have it, can with great difficulty be persuaded to grasp and wield it.

But they who really understand and obey this passage will act differently. They, into whose hands God has not committed the sword, will, of course, let it alone, and rather suffer all things than presume so far as to take it; and this, because they recognize the command of Christ and the ordinance of God, which they feel certain dare not be trifled with, and against the violation of which they guard as against the executioner, the gallows or the wheel. And they, to whom God has given the sword, will cheerfully and fearlessly sway it over one and all, regardless of their subjects' station and property; for they know that they are bound to check scandal wherever they meet it, and, therefore, they obey God and serve Him eagerly. This must suffice for the first point.

The question which we stated in the beginning now claims attention. As private persons are absolutely forbidden to grasp the sword, and the Lord reproves Peter for drawing his sword in Christ's behalf, would it then be lawful for a government to defend itself when attacked on account of religion? Or, in plainer terms: considering that Christ did not permit Peter to rescue Him with the sword, are rulers permitted to resist attacks made on the Gospel, and to instruct their subjects everywhere to defend it with the sword?

It is necessary here, first, to observe the distinction between the civil government, the office of the ministry, and the private person. The civil government, above all other duties assigned to it, has received the emphatic command to disseminate and apply God's Word, and with the sword to protect those subjects who are oppressed on account of the Word. About this there is no question whatever; for the sword must protect virtue and punish vice, and, above all, serve to promote the knowledge of God, as we infer from Rom. 13. And God says in Isa.: The Church shall "suck the breasts of kings," that is, they shall be her protectors; and, in the 24. Ps.: "Lift up your heads, O ye gates; and be ye lifted up, ye everlasting doors; and the King of glory shall come in."

But ministers of the Gospel and private persons are not the civil government; therefore, neither ministers nor private persons dare draw the sword, for they have received no command to this effect. Peter, at that time, did not understand this so; for he did not know that the ministry would be an office void of royal and princely favor. Peter should not, therefore, have drawn the sword. But all temporal authorities are obliged to shield God's Word and the true Church. Had God ordained them as swineherds, then their only duty would be to protect the throats and care for the corn of their subjects; but, as it now is, they must, first of all, preserve the honor and knowledge of God in the human race, perpetuate the true worship of God, punish and exterminate false doctrine and idolatry, and rather hazard everything than suffer themselves or their subjects to be forced into idolatry or falsehood. Therefore the 2. Ps. says to them: "Kiss the Son," that is, receive and protect God's Word!

This is the civil ruler's noblest duty. We see in history that God imposed this duty, and that the Holy Spirit highly extols not only the pious Jewish kings, Jehoshaphat, Josiah, Hezekiah, but also the kings of the Gentiles, e.g. Nebuchadnezzar, Darius, Cyrus, because they instituted the true worship of God and violently opposed the worship of idols.

This being the office of the civil government, it follows that she must, as long as she can, protect and preserve herself and those belonging to her against the attacks of the ungodly and never give way to these assaults; for it is impossible that they who persecute God's Word and carry on idolatry, should have the Holy Ghost. For what would be the result should she refuse to do this? She alone bears the sword; and her subjects dare not take it even in case she herself refuses to use it. The inevitable result must be that success would crown the efforts of the wicked, the Word of God would be extirpated, God's pure worship would cease, and the old idolatry would be re-established!

Now who is willing to sanction this and, by sanctioning it, to heap upon himself such great and terrible sin? yes, who will dare to do this, knowing that it is written: "Kiss the Son, lest He be angry, and ye perish from the way;" further, Lev. 24: "He that blasphemeth the name of the Lord, he shall surely be put to death;" also: "Flee from idolatry;" and again: "Rulers are a terror to evil works?" And now, since the establishing of idolatry is an evil work, they who have the sword are not only permitted, but also seriously commanded, with all boldness to shield and save themselves and theirs from this evil by the sword. On the subject of self-defense, you may find the answer to the question, whether subordinates may defend themselves against those superiors who exercise public tyranny, as against notorious murderers or highwaymen, by reading the Admonition to the German People, and other works which specially treat on this subject; it would occupy too much time at present.

But here we speak of those alone who have the sword, that is, who are in office. Now if bishops, for instance, who are of that class of people that has not the sword, deprive their subjects of one of the elements in the Holy Supper, or inflict upon them other manifest errors, these subjects, although they ought, in such cases, to obey God rather than men, and although God seriously requires such disobedience to their commands, dare not draw the sword on account of such errors, but must bear them, if they would not use the sword like Peter, who had not been commanded to do so.

But you say that a Christian must tolerate injustice and violence, and not oppose them by force. I answer that the subject of which we now are speaking is the civil government, who is the sword-bearer; and she has sufficient violence done her when other governments destroy her peace and attack her in war. Let us regard these her sufferings as severe enough, and not impose still further burdens upon a Christian government! He who afflicts her still more, and even snatches the sword out of her hand, virtually gives his consent that the enemies of truth shall exercise their malice without restraint, and even deprive us of God's Word. There is time enough for giving such consent, when the government is not able to protect the truth. But as long as we can hope for her help, and as long as the matter depends upon the help of God and reposes in His hand, it is our duty to venture and to suffer, so that we may not be accused of being more mindful of favor, peace, and the like, than of God's Word and the salvation and well-being of the subjects.

Ever clear and plain, therefore, stands the command: *Osculamini filium; Hunc audite*, "Kiss the Son;" "Hear ye Him;" "Flee from idolatry," &c. Such commands as these require of the worldly ruler that he oppose not merely worldly or temporal offence, but also false doctrine and false worship. But by what means must he do this? What means has God given him? Read St. Paul's 13. chapter to the Romans, where you are informed: "He beareth not the sword in vain." But against whom shall he bear it? Against those who defend false doctrines and idolatry, and who seek to compel others to accept heresy and false worship. This the Christian government dare not tolerate. For the heavenly Lord of lords has forbidden it, and declares that God is worshiped and His Word lauded when we jeopard peace, the favor of men, and the like, rather than sanction that which militates against God's Word.

This, then, is the import of Peter's unauthorized attempt at liberating the Lord by fighting with the sword. But in our text we find yet another sermon, which is a reproof designed especially for the Jews, who had been instructed by their proper government to take swords and staves, and with them to attack the Lord Jesus. Still they receive the Lord's reprimand. "Are ye come out as against a thief with swords and staves for to take me? I sat daily with you teaching in the temple, and ye laid no hold on me."

With these words the Lord rebukes them for a twofold reason. In the first place, even when the civil government puts the sword into her subjects' hands, they must not take it if they are expected to use it in an unrighteous cause; and, secondly, they should not have taken it to use it against Him, their Lord. For He was no murderer. It was the doctrine that was in question. Doctrinal disputes are not to be judged and decided by fire and sword in imitation of the Papists, but according to the Scriptures. If we are heretics, as they accuse us, then let them prove it from Scripture, and leave the hangman at home; he has no business with such disputes.

But as the Jews dealt with Christ, so the Papists, their disciples, still deal with Him. They can not and they will not enter upon a debate, unless their doctors and papal decrees are recognized as having equal authority with God's Word. But since we refuse to recognize them as having such, they come out against us with swords and staves, as did the Jews against Christ. I suppose they do this so that every one can see that they are of the same breed with the Jews, to whom the Lord says, Jno. 8: "Ye are of your father the devil," for "ye seek to kill me." This applies admirably to these bloodhounds, the Papists. But we, who, like Peter, have not been called to use the sword, must suffer these things. God, however, in His own good time, will punish such cruel despotism, and mercifully deliver His own from the fury of these blood-thirsty tyrants. Amen.

4

The Lord Jesus Led to Annas and Caiaphas and Tried by the Jews

Those who had arrested Jesus took him to Caiaphas the high priest, where the teachers of the law and the elders had assembled. But Peter followed him at a distance, right up to the courtyard of the high priest. He entered and sat down with the guards to see the outcome. The chief priests and the whole Sanhedrin were looking for false evidence against Jesus so that they could put him to death. But they did not find any, though many false witnesses came forward. Finally two came forward and declared, "This fellow said, 'I am able to destroy the temple of God and rebuild it in three days.'" Then the high priest stood up and said to Jesus, "Are you not going to answer? What is this testimony that these men are bringing against you?" But Jesus remained silent. The high priest said to him, "I charge you under oath by the living God: Tell us if you are the Messiah, the Son of God." "You have said so," Jesus replied. "But I say to all of you: From now on you will see the Son of Man sitting at the right hand of the Mighty One and coming on the clouds of heaven." Then the high priest tore his clothes and said, "He has spoken blasphemy! Why do we need any more witnesses? Look, now you have heard the blasphemy. What do you think?" "He is worthy of death," they answered. Then they spit in his face and struck him with their fists. Others slapped him and said, "Prophesy to us, Messiah. Who hit you?"

—MATTHEW 26:57–68

We have heard how our Lord Jesus was betrayed by Judas in the garden and taken by the Jews. Now we come to notice how He was brought before Caiaphas, the high priest, under such charges as to lead to the unanimous decision that there was sufficient cause for delivering Him to Pilate and aiming at His life.

In describing these things so carefully it was not the only object of the Evangelists to teach us the holy innocence of our Lord Jesus. That He was wholly pure and altogether without sin we must conclude from the known fact that He was the Son of God, conceived by the Holy Ghost, and born of the Virgin Mary. But, since the Church and the Gospel must receive the same treatment in the world which the Lord Jesus received, the history of Christ's wrongs is given us especially to the end that we may not be offended when similar wrongs are inflicted upon us also, but that we may always refer to it for consolation and learn to be patient. For if God's Son, our Master and our Head, was falsely accused, delivered to Pilate by the high priests, scribes and elders, and surrendered to the Gentiles to be crucified, is it to be wondered at if we receive similar treatment? The servant is not to be more successful than his master. Therefore, we should rejoice when our experience is such that we can truthfully boast: This was the experience of my Lord Jesus also. For if we are like Him in suffering, we are warranted in the hope of being like Him in glory too; yea, and even before the revelation of this glory, we shall, in our suffering, derive from Him comfort, aid, deliverance. This history, which shows that even our Lord Jesus was not exempt from suffering, serves, therefore, first, to minister unto us consolation, that we may become more cheerful and more patient in our sufferings.

And, secondly, it offers us an antidote against the common offences of this world. For every one regards the titular dignitaries, called chief priests and elders of the people here, as pious men and saints, in virtue of their office, station and pomp. And so to-day the Pope, bishops, monks and priests desire, on account of their office, to be looked upon and treated as the most eminent members of the Christian Church. But let us learn here not to judge men by the office they hold, else we shall be deceived; but by the manner in which they act towards Christ—by the relation which their heart, their will, sustains towards Him. When, by this text, we find good or evil in them, we must judge them accordingly; for then our judgement shall always be just. The office is, without a doubt, a holy and a good one; but he who holds it may be a villain. For here we see that the high priests, the scribes and the elders, who are the rulers and leaders of the people in spiritual things and in things temporal, are the very ones who cannot tolerate the Lord Jesus and who, by dint of unremitting persecution and manifold intrigues, finally bring Him to the cross. We must confess that they are God's worst enemies and also, as Luke testifies in the 5. chapter of Acts, Epicureans, who in those days said that there is no resurrection from the dead, neither angel nor spirit. If we would, therefore, know to a certainty whether Pope, bishops, and the like, are pious or not, we must not be misled by their office; but need merely see how they conduct themselves towards the Gospel and the true doctrine, when we shall find that all of them are disciples of Judas, and that their hearts are disposed towards the Gospel as were those of the high priests towards Christ. These are the very fruits by which we may know the false prophets, the wolves, even when they come in sheep's clothing and have the appearance of devout and harmless persons.

We shall now take up the trial of our Lord, and see with what hatred, malignity, craft, and virulence they treat Christ.

The Evangelist John mentions that the Jews led the Lord Jesus first to Annas, who, according to Acts 4., was also a high priest, but not in that year, and who was the father-in-law to Caiaphas, who officiated at the time. But Annas soon gave Him over to his son-in-law, Caiaphas, who was the high priest that same year; for with him the chief priests and elders were already assembled.

Here we see, in the first place, how inequitably the high priests deal with the Lord Jesus; for they are at the same time both plaintiff and judge. The Lord could, therefore, not receive justice, let His cause have been ever so good, and let Him have said and done what He would. Such a way of proceeding would be very dishonorable in a worldly law-suit, in which the same person is forbidden to act as plaintiff and judge by a special law. But nothing is sinful for these holy ones; they have all power; they can do as they please, and think they have the right to do so! Woe to him who construes their actions ill, tells them they are in the wrong, or admonishes them!

Just so our spiritless tyrants, Pope, cardinals and bishops conduct themselves. The Pope has for many successive years been causing us Germans to gape in expectation of a Council, at which, as he has been pretending, he would abolish the dissension existing in religious matters.

And, on our part, many serious efforts have been made at many an imperial diet, and on other occasions, to secure a free, Christian Council, at which to end the present disunion by means of the Holy Scriptures. But it is the manifest desire of the Pope to treat us and the Gospel as the Jews here treated Christ. He is a party in the case; accusation is brought against the blasphemous dogmas and counterfeit cultus which he has insinuated into the Church, in spite of God's Word, and upon which he still insists; what should he, as the defendant, do? If he himself is to be the judge, he will not declare himself in the wrong and decide in favor of his opponent, the plaintiff. But upon such a course as this the Pope and his parasites—these honorable men!—strenuously insist. Yea and more, when a Council is held he takes public part in it, while we, previously condemned by him, obtain neither vote nor seat. This is a wanton, unjust and grievous procedure.

But here we have the proof that the world does not desire and is not able to deal otherwise with Christ. We should, therefore, be resigned, and, with the Lord Jesus, bear such injustice until the appointed time; for what else can we do? Caiaphas, who, as judge, sat in the judgment seat, himself accuses the Lord Jesus and then even decides against Him. This is the first act of injustice in the trial before the priests.

Another atrocious feature of this trial we find in their absolutely demanding the death of the Lord Jesus, while they cannot find sufficient cause for this, but must call to their assistance falsehood and false witnesses, until finally Caiaphas, the judge, himself arises and brings forth an accusation possessing some semblance of foundation. Among other false testimony submitted, was that of "two false witnesses," who came "and said: This fellow said, I am able to destroy the temple of God, and to build it in three days."

The correct history of this latter charge we find in the 2. chapter of John. When our Lord Jesus, in Jerusalem, at the first passover after His baptism, had with a scourge driven out of the temple the changers of money and the merchants, together with their oxen, sheep, doves, and whatever else they had, and poured out the changers' money, and overthrown the tables, the Jews gathered together and said: Thou venturest to exercise special violence here; hast Thou authority to do this? What sign shewest Thou unto us, seeing that Thou doest these things? Then the Lord answered them thus:

"Destroy this temple, and in three days I will raise it up." By this He meant to say the same as by the sign of the Prophet Jonah, Matt. 12., namely this: You desire a sign and shall have it. You shall kill me; but on the third day I will raise myself from the dead. He for whom such sign does not suffice is past all help. This is the narrative.

But see, how wantonly they pervert His words! He says: "Destroy this temple;" and then they charge Him with having said: "I am able to destroy the temple," thus to make Him appear guilty of having spoken against the temple of God. And even if we accept the Jews' interpretation of Christ's words, admitting that they were spoken with reference to the temple at Jerusalem, would a man be guilty of death on account of using such words? In short, he who would make charges against Christ, must first become a base liar; our Papists also are a living proof of this. What they cry out against the Gospel is bare falsehood. They are dead to every sense of shame, daub their notions into other men's books and belie us, saying that the holy sacrament receives scandalous treatment at our hands, that we throw against the wall what remains of the cup, and that we tramp with our feet what is left of the consecrated bread. Are these not gross, palpable lies? Why, common bread and wine is not treated so, but is preserved. How much more would we then not keep decently that, of which we confess and teach, in opposition to the Sacramentarians, that it is not mere bread and not mere wine, but the true body and blood of Christ, given for us upon the cross and shed for our sins! But we need not wonder at the Papists' lies. He who deals in falsehoods can speak no truth, and he who acts contrary to truth cannot help himself except with lies. On this principle the world, as we here see, dealt with Christ, and will continue so to deal with the Christians and the Holy Gospel; for it cannot do otherwise.

But when their witness agreed not together and was powerless in itself, Caiaphas, the judge or high priest, rushed to the rescue, and, according to John, asked Jesus of His disciples, and of His doctrine, as though he would say: What is this new doctrine Thou bringest? Art Thou dissatisfied with Moses? Must Thou have something extra? Art Thou alone wise and are all we fools? Where are they now who regarded Thy doctrine right and divine? It may be such a good doctrine that we too would be pleased with it and receive it. But it is merely the rabble, which knows nothing about the law, that Thou attachest to thyself; the honest and upright desire not thy preaching. To such question the Lord answered: "I ever taught in the synagogue, and in the temple, whither the Jews always resort; and in secret have I said nothing. Why askest thou me? ask them which heard me, what I have said unto them; behold, they know what I said." The Lord does not desire His doctrine to be despised, and says that He had not feared the light, but had preached it openly to the world, that it should, therefore, not be reviled as a thing done in a corner.

When He had thus spoken, a scoundrel standing by dealt the Lord a severe blow with the palm of his hand, as though it were intolerable that the high priest should be thus answered and not more reverently treated. Even to-day we see such priests' slaves, who are ready to defend with the sword the sacrilegious doctrines and shameful, sodomitical life of the Pope and his shaved and shorn train. And then we also find those vain prattlers, jesters, mountebanks, and the like, who would serve them faithfully, and whose only object in blaspheming and reviling the holy Gospel is, to receive the favor of their bishops and of the idol at Rome. This we must suffer, indeed, as Christ also suffered it, but dare not connive at it, nor forbear rebuking and publishing such vice. We must do as Christ here does: He addresses the servant, and tells him that he had smitten Him unjustly, but does nothing further.

When they now found themselves without any cause of action, Caiaphas, the high priest, comes to the main point, saying: "I adjure Thee by the living God, that Thou tell us whether Thou be the Christ, the Son of God." Knave Caiaphas thinks thus to hit the nail on the head, and to seize the Lord Jesus by the throat. Observe here, first of all, that it is not the intention of Caiaphas that he or the rest should believe in the Lord, in case He should say that He is the Christ. By no means! But this is the very confession they desire to hear Him make, thinking that then they could convict Him without difficulty. And Christ understands them well enough; but this does not induce Him to deny who He is. He answers: "Thou hast said," that is, just as thou hast said, I am the Christ And what is still more, it shall only be a little while yet and ye shall "see the Son of man sitting on the right hand of power;" that is, after these days I shall not need to suffer any more, but, in my glorified body, shall show that I am not only a man, as you regard me, but also the almighty Son of God, who rules over all, and on the judgment day I shall come in the clouds of heaven and judge the quick and the dead.

Behold, now the high priest has heard the glorious, excellent confession which tells him what he should believe concerning this man, whom he and others had prepared themselves to entrap, and whom they were resolved on killing. Let us see what use the high priest makes of this confession. Matthew tells us that he "rent his clothes, saying, He hath spoken blasphemy; what further need have we of witnesses? Behold, now ye have heard His blasphemy. What think ye?"

In this, the first trial of our blessed Lord Jesus, which took place in the house of Caiaphas, He was declared a heretic and blasphemer. This gluts the high priestly maw; and now it only remains to have some worldly accusation brought against Christ before Pilate, so that His death might be decreed. While each one privately deliberates on this, our innocent Lord Jesus is made to submit to their scorn; He must suffer them to spit in His holy face, and Himself to be buffeted, derided, smitten and mocked. For they regard such treatment altogether just, because Christ has been pronounced a heretic and blasphemer. They make a jest of His saying that He is the Christ. One strikes Him on this side, another on that. "Aha! You are the Christ, are you," they say, "then, pray, prophesy unto us, who is he that smote Thee?"

But let us diligently mark whether the Gospel does not fare in the same way to-day. The Papists question us, and desire to know our doctrine. And then, when we with the greatest simplicity and honesty confess our doctrine, as was done at Augsburg, at Ratisbon, and at imperial diets in other places, the mighty clamor rises: Heretics, heretics! All are busy then at heaping upon the poor Christians whatever ignominy, contempt, mockery and injury they can rally. They cry: It is Evangelical you are, is it? Is this your Gospel? Just wait, we will give you a little of the Gospel? And so they have gone to work and inflicted a most atrocious reproduction of the Passion-History upon the pious Christians of Germany, Italy, France and England.

It is, therefore, important that we carefully study this priestly *Processum Juris*. For then, in case we are brought before a similar tribunal, we can follow the example of our Lord Jesus, learning of Him patience, and deriving from Him true consolation. And, should we be compelled to suffer with Him for the sake of His Word, we can hope also to live with Him, and with Him to be lifted to glory. May God grant this to us all. Amen.

5

Peter Thrice Denies the Lord Jesus in the House of Caiaphas

Now Peter was sitting out in the courtyard, and a servant girl came to him. "You also were with Jesus of Galilee," she said. But he denied it before them all. "I don't know what you're talking about," he said. Then he went out to the gateway, where another servant girl saw him and said to the people there, "This fellow was with Jesus of Nazareth." He denied it again, with an oath: "I don't know the man!" After a little while, those standing there went up to Peter and said, "Surely you are one of them; your accent gives you away." Then he began to call down curses, and he swore to them, "I don't know the man!" Immediately a rooster crowed. Then Peter remembered the word Jesus had spoken: "Before the rooster crows, you will disown me three times." And he went outside and wept bitterly.

—**MATTHEW 26:69–75**

This is a useful narrative, for which reason it is related by each of the four Evangelists. It is useful chiefly in two respects. First, it teaches us to cherish humility and avoid presumption; for see how easily Peter, who would previously have gladly imperiled his body and his life for the Lord Jesus, is brought to such a terrible fall. And secondly, it teaches us how we may regain grace, after we have fallen into sin; for Peter furnishes us with a pleasing example of Christian repentance, showing what repentance really is, and how we must be freed from sin. But let us first relate the history.

When Jesus was taken captive in the garden and led away, first to Annas, father-in-law to Caiaphas, and from Annas to the high priest Caiaphas, John, as he himself writes, followed from afar and entered the house of Caiaphas, in which he was acquainted, bringing Peter in with him. The latter sat down with the servants in the house and warmed himself at the fire. Then a damsel asked him whether he was a disciple of the captive Jesus. He vehemently denied that he was. The cock then crew for the first time. Upon this, as Matthew and Mark relate, Peter went away from the fire, out into the porch, where he was encountered in a similar way by a maid, who began to say to them that stood by, This is one of them. Luke tells us that it was a man who said this of Peter. It needs merely be remembered here that, after the maid had begun to speak about Peter, the rest also expressed their opinions and chimed in with the maid. Peter then a second time denied. And finally, about the space of one hour after, as we are informed by Luke, he was met by one of the servants of the high priest, who, according to John, was a kinsman to him whose ear Peter cut off. He attacks Peter a little more severely than the rest, publicly saying that he had seen him in the garden with Jesus. Peter would not keep silent to this accusation, for he feared that it would endanger his life. Then began he to curse and to swear, saying, I know not the man, of whom ye speak. Now the Lord turns and casts upon Peter a look which so penetrates his soul, that he now perceives what he has done; and he goes out of Caiaphas' palace and weeps bitterly. This is about the whole of the occurrence in order, as related by the four Evangelists.

Here we should, in the first place, as stated in the beginning, learn from the example of pious Peter to recognize our weakness, so that we may refrain from putting absolute confidence in other people or in ourselves. For our hearts are so entirely faint and fickle that they change every hour, as the Lord says in the 2. chapter of John. Who in the world would have expected such instability and feebleness in Peter! When the Lord, Luke 22., cautioned him, saying, Satan hath desired to have you, that he may sift you as wheat, how courageous was he not, how bold and undismayed! "Lord," said he, "I am ready to go with Thee, both into prison, and to death." And when the Lord continued to admonish him, telling him not to be so foolhardy, and that before the cock would crow twice he should have denied Him thrice, we see that Peter thought it all a fable. He imagined this impossible, and intended to adhere to and defend the Lord at the risk of his own life. And his actions, indeed, show this to have been his intention. For in the hour of greatest peril, when the Jews were taking captive the Lord in the garden, Peter was the first to draw his sword, and he slashed into the mob, notwithstanding that he and only one other armed person opposed so many who were well equipped. Now who would have believed that one so valiant, who so faithfully stands by his Master, would so soon afterwards shamefully betray Him? In the garden no one attempted to hurt Peter and his fellow disciples, for the Lord's "Let these go" protected them. And especially here in the house of Caiaphas no one desires to injure them. But when, altogether incidentally, and perhaps through sympathy, the damsel that kept the door said unto Peter: "Art not thou also one of this man's disciples?" his courage failed him, and he feared that he would have to share his Master's fate if he should answer yes, and, therefore, he denies that he is a disciple. And when he was accosted on this point the second time and the third, he began to curse and to swear, calling upon God to visit upon him His wrath if he had ever known or seen the man.

Let us pay due attention to the conduct of Peter, so that we may learn properly to know ourselves and other people, and to beware of presumptuousness. For if such a denial of faith can proceed from Peter, who, above all the other disciples, had a heart filled with loyalty and love for the Lord Jesus, yea, who was so enlightened by the grace of God that even Christ said unto him: "Blessed art thou, Simon, for flesh and blood hath not revealed it unto thee, but my Father which is in heaven," and that He gave to him the name Cephas, "a stone," how much more easily can not such denial come from us poor mortals, who are much inferior to Peter in point of gifts, and, in all other respects, much more faint and frail? Be on thy guard, therefore; be not irreverently bold; think not that thou hast climbed the mountain and art out of danger; remember that thy flesh is totally corrupt! Neither doth Satan slumber, but walketh about as a roaring lion, seeking whose heart he may trouble, and whom he may cast down or even devour. Therefore, be vigilant; live in the fear of God; build upon His grace alone, and in Him repose thy trust and confidence! And let that which Jesus spake in the garden to Peter, James and John, "Watch and pray, that ye enter not into temptation," be spoken also unto thee, that thou mayest neither snore nor be falsely secure, as though there were no danger and no need for fear from henceforth, but that thou mayest watch and be sober, not doubting that thy arch-enemy is close at hand, yea, that thou bearest him in thy bosom! Thou wouldst, therefore, be lost, should

God not stand by thee with His Holy Spirit. Thou canst neither govern nor restrain thyself one single hour. Therefore, say: I will pray God to give me His Holy Spirit, that He may rule and rightly lead me, and either ward off disturbance and temptation, or else graciously succor me and suffer me not to fall! This is the first point presented by our narrative. Under this head, however, appropriately comes the solemn admonition of the Lord, given in the 21. chapter of Luke: "Take heed to yourselves, lest at any time your hearts be overcharged with surfeiting, and drunkenness;" for we are just as ill-bred as the brute, which, when well fed, shows its insolence. He who has plenty and to spare, readily forgets God and His Word, or else cares very little for them; and then, before he knows it, he is entangled in the devil's net. Therefore, wouldst thou be out of danger, observe these three things: fear God, be watchful and sober, and pray without ceasing! For, although we must still feel temptation's thrusts, and sometimes fall because of weakness, God, through His Holy Spirit, will lift us up again, and not suffer us to remain victims of temptation.

In the second place, we find consolation in this narrative. Here we clearly see the fruit of our Lord Jesus' sufferings; and Peter's conduct plainly pictures to us not only the grace and mercy of God, but also the way in which grace may be regained by us when lost in unrighteousness and sin. Terrible and heinous is the fall of Peter; as such he feels it most forcibly, and, therefore, he cannot longer bear to mingle with men, but steals away and weeps bitterly.

But here we find that the Lord not only foretold to him his fall, but afterwards also received him into favor without punishing him as his sin had deserved. For on Easter, before the Lord Jesus had shown Himself, the angel who was at the grave commanded the women to announce to His disciples, and to Peter especially, that the Lord had risen. And the Lord Himself, soon after He had appeared to Magdalene and the other women, appeared to Peter and comforted him. This all works together for our consolation, teaching us not to banish from our hearts confidence in God's grace, though we may have fallen, but, seeing how the Lord deals with Peter, to be assured that He has died on our account, and that His sufferings shall bring us consolation and assistance, although we are poor sinners. For if sinners are not to have the benefit of the sufferings of Christ, then would He have rejected His disciples, and particularly Peter, first of all, and nevermore have interested Himself for them, because they were all offended because of Him, fled from Him, and so shamefully denied Him. But the merciful Lord does not so; they are still His dear disciples, notwithstanding that they disgraced their calling. Let us mark this and apply it to our hearts for consolation; for thus will our gracious God also deal with us.

But, say you, what becomes of poor Judas? Do we not see him cut off from all grace? Although we shall come to speak of this hereafter, it is still necessary for us, in this connection, to know what it was that furthered and preserved Peter, and what it was that subjected Judas to impediments and despair, so that Peter's case may teach us how to take care of ourselves and how to beware of that which befell Judas. Now we must make a distinction between Peter and Judas with reference to the heinousness of their crimes. For, while both transgress the will of God and subject themselves to everlasting condemnation, Judas' sin is greater than that of Peter. Judas surrenders to sin voluntarily and with premeditation, and, notwithstanding the Lord's frequent and fervent warnings, prefers his sins above Christ's love. This is not the case with Peter; his sin was accidental, not deliberate and malicious; his denial of Christ was the result of casual diffidence or weakness. Had he apprehended this result, he would not have entered the house of Caiaphas. Then, there is this further distinction between Peter and Judas, that the former, unlike the latter, is not the enemy of Christ and does not hate Him; that he does not run counter to the Lord, like the latter, with such wanton scorn, hatred and obstinacy that no exhortation to penitence and no favor of the Lord can influence him to repent; but that, before he considers and perceives what he is doing, through fear and weakness he is so overcome that he denies his dear Lord and begins to curse and to swear.

Let us mark well the aforenamed distinction in regard to sins, viz.: that, although both Peter and Judas do sin, and thus subject themselves to the judgment of God, the sin of Judas is more enormous than the sin of Peter. For the Lord subsequently makes the difference between Pilate and the Jews, saying, Jno. 19., "He that hath delivered me unto thee hath the greater sin." This is the reason why the conscience of Judas is more painfully wounded than Peter's, and his sufferings are more severe; the burden borne by Judas is by far the heavier and the more oppressive. Nevertheless, Peter's sin had deserved death, as well as that of Judas.

This distinction is justified also by St. Paul, who says of his persecuting Christ and His believers that he had done this in ignorance, and that, although his work of persecution was a damnable, mortal sin, it was still not at all to be compared with the persecutions carried on by the chief priests and Pharisees. This difference deserves to be diligently regarded, so that we may beware of such wanton and malicious sins as of a most grievous burden, and therefore watch that we do not obstinately persevere in impenitence. Now, although sins may be classified according to the degree of their criminality, and although no doubt exists that the greater the sin, the greater the consequent torment of conscience; still, when a man has obtained knowledge of his sins and is terrified by the wrath of God, he must not judge the measure of forgiveness and grace by the enormity or number of his sins. All sins, even the least, are so great and serious that we are not able to estimate their heinousness; yea, so great that we could not endure one of them, were it adequately seen and felt by us. Besides, Satan can so magnify a sin, though it be not the greatest, that the timid, fearful soul which is guilty of it supposes that no one else on earth has ever committed so grievous a crime. Therefore, we must know and hold fast the Gospel doctrine of the grace and kindness of the Son of God; for this tells us that grace is mightier than all sin. It is the great object of God's Word and promises that no one may despond or despair on account of sin but that all may trust in the grace of God through His only begotten Son, our Lord Jesus.

On this point Judas and Peter differ. Judas looks only at the enormity of his sins, falls into despair, thinks that all eternity can afford him neither counsel nor aid, and then the poor fellow goes and hangs himself. And why? Simply because he had despised God's Word and had not been bettered by it. When he now stood in need of consolation, but did not have the Word and desired not to turn to the Lord Jesus in faith, he was beyond all reach of help. Peter also wept bitterly, and feared and trembled on account of his sins, but he had more diligently heard and better remembered the Word of the Lord Jesus. Therefore, when he now finds himself in distress, he makes use of the Word, thinks of that which Christ has told him, clings to this, consoles himself with it, and hopes that God will be merciful to him. In such misery this is the true relief, which poor Judas lacked. But that this was really the course Peter took, and that he did abide by God's Word and grace, the Lord testifies in the 22. chapter of Luke, saying: "I have prayed for thee, that thy faith fail not." While he was denying Christ, we do not see that there was a spark of faith in his heart; but afterwards, when his conscience was aroused and he was tortured by it, his faith returned, preserving to him this Word of Christ, and preventing him from falling into despair.

Let us then learn here what true repentance is. Peter "wept bitterly." In this way repentance begins; the heart must truly perceive sin and be sincerely sorry for it, so that our delight in it, our love for it, and our living in it may cease. Our having disobeyed God's will and sinned, must be for us a source of heartfelt affliction.

Our might, however, cannot bring this about; but the Lord calls us to repent and makes His face to shine again upon us, just as He here calls and admonishes Peter by the crowing of the cock, of which He had told him before, and by turning and looking upon him. For we are by nature so disposed that we delight in sin and take pleasure in committing it continually. We see this in the case of Peter; for, after he had denied Christ once, he still keeps on until he has denied Him thrice, and cursed and sworn: "I do not know the man," being concerned about nothing. But when the cock crows and the Lord turns to look upon him, Peter immediately pauses and considers what he has done. Now, according to our nature and to the nature of sin, sin cannot help but terrify us, threaten us with God's wrath, and fill our hearts with anguish, as was the case with both Peter and Judas. Judas, when he perceived his sin, became so uneasy that he did not know what to do with himself. And Peter's agony was so great that it compelled him to flee from his fellow-men and give vent to his grief in tears, of which he could not shed enough.

When we feel such terror and anguish our best course is, first, to humble ourselves before God and freely confess our sins: O God, I am indeed a poor, miserable sinner, and, shouldst Thou depart from me with Thy grace, am able only to sin; and then, to abide God's Word and promises, adding:

"But be merciful to me for the sake of Thy Son, Jesus Christ!" When the soul thus seeks to console itself with God's Word, and sincerely trusts that God, for His Son's sake, will be merciful, then must the anguish abate and comfort surely follow. True and complete repentance, then, is this: to be terrified and humbled by sin, and to find comfort in the Lord Jesus and His sufferings through faith.

Thus, no doubt, Peter consoled himself with the word spoken to him by the Lord at the passover: "Satan hath desired to have you, but I have prayed for thee, that thy faith fail not," Luke 22. For, although his heart was filled with anxiety and sorrow, he did not despair like Judas. True, at first this consolation was as small as a grain of mustard-seed. But since the ground, on which this little consolation rested, was God's own Word and promises, it increased wonderfully, and when Peter met Christ again, on holy Easter-day, it had grown so great that all terrors and all doubts had fled, and nothing remained except heart-felt humility, with which to confess his weakness and cheerfully to acknowledge himself a sinner. Sin was not able to leave aught in Peter's heart except this weakness and this confession. This consolation, like a mighty deluge, suffocated, yea, quenched the fire that had threatened to consume his heart. Since, therefore, we cannot live without temptation, we should prepare for it in time, and especially with diligence hear God's Word, and practice and remember it, so that consolation, like Peter's, may be ours in time of sorrow.

Thus we find that this example of St. Peter is given us for instruction and for consolation. We should learn from it, first, to flee false security and to live in the fear of God; for it is an easy matter even for great saints terribly to fall. But, secondly, we must also learn from this example to cling to God's Word, and to draw comfort from it, even when we have fallen, so that we may not, like Judas, despair on account of sin. For God does not wish any one to exalt himself on account of his endowments, for which reason we all should fear, watch and pray; neither does He, on the other hand, wish any one to be driven into despair by his sins. The Son of God became man and died upon the cross for the very purpose of banishing such evils. Therefore, if thou wouldst be a true Christian, fear God and confide in His grace and Word, and thou shalt always find consolation, deliverance and help. May our dear Father in Heaven, through His Holy

Spirit, grant this to us all, for the sake of our blessed Lord and Saviour. Amen.

6

Christ is Delivered to Pilate.— Judas Hangs Himself.— The Potter's Field

Early in the morning, all the chief priests and the elders of the people made their plans how to have Jesus executed. So they bound him, led him away and handed him over to Pilate the governor. When Judas, who had betrayed him, saw that Jesus was condemned, he was seized with remorse and returned the thirty pieces of silver to the chief priests and the elders. "I have sinned," he said, "for I have betrayed innocent blood." "What is that to us?" they replied. "That's your responsibility." So Judas threw the money into the temple and left. Then he went away and hanged himself. The chief priests picked up the coins and said, "It is against the law to put this into the treasury, since it is blood money." So they decided to use the money to buy the potter's field as a burial place for foreigners. That is why it has been called the Field of Blood to this day. Then what was spoken by Jeremiah the prophet was fulfilled: "They took the thirty pieces of silver, the price set on him by the people of Israel, and they used them to buy the potter's field, as the Lord commanded me."
—**MATTHEW 27:1–10**

You have heard, my friends, how the Lord Jesus was first led to Annas, who then sent Him bound to Caiaphas, where the chief priests and scribes were assembled, and where these latter and the entire council sought false witness against Him, and finally falsely accused Him of blasphemy, for which, they said, He ought to die. We expect to speak further on this hereafter.

Next we find Him brought before Pilate; we shall see what happened there. But before we speak of this, we ought to know what was, after all, the reason why the chief spiritual and temporal rulers at Jerusalem were so highly incensed and imbittered against the Lord that they flock together by night, make inquisition concerning Him at an unseasonable hour, and are in such uneasy haste to have Him destroyed, at the same time being unable to allege aught against Him except invented lies. It would be too lengthy, however, to relate all this now; each one can read it for himself in the history written by the four Evangelists, or learn it during the year from the preaching of the Word at Church. The Lord Jesus excuses neither the doctrine nor the life of these men, but censures both severely. Thus He calls them "an evil and adulterous generation," a "generation of vipers," and not the children of God, which they boast themselves to be, but "the children of the devil," because they can neither speak, teach, nor do that which is good. And shortly previous to this time, before He was taken, He gave them a final rebuke, calling down upon them, Matt. 23., the eight times uttered "woe!" And this it was that enkindled their hatred into such consuming flames, that lent cruelty to their enmity, and that made them so impetuous in the pursuit of their object, that Christ, being now in their power, had no opportunity to escape. Still, in order to give their savage, murderous hatred a plausible appearance, that is, to make it seem that their law fully authorized them to kill Christ, the high priest, as the Evangelists write, when he heard Christ say: "Hereafter shall ye see the Son of man sitting on the right hand of power, and coming in the clouds of heaven," rent his clothes and said: "He hath spoken blasphemy; what further need have we of witnesses? behold, now ye have heard His blasphemy. What think ye?" And all the others who were present said: "He is guilty of death." Soon after this they began to treat the dear Lord Jesus most miserably, not one among them having compassion on Him, but all of them enraged against Him like raving lions. The 22. and other Psalms tell us about this.

One thing, however, was still in their way. They knew very well that Pilate would care very little for that which they deemed sufficient cause for death; for He was a Gentile and had not received command of the Roman Emperor to execute the Jews because of their faith,—else he would have had to destroy all of them. For this reason they assembled when the morning was come, and, as Matthew writes, "took counsel against Jesus to put Him to death," that is, they considered what accusation they would bring against

Him before Pilate. For they knew well enough that Pilate would not slay Christ on account of His having blasphemed in the judgment of the Jews. They found it necessary, therefore, to devise some specious, civil charge to be presented to Pilate, who was a temporal judge. For, by saying that Christ was a blasphemer, they could not have broken His neck.

Let us here see and learn how quick and venomous Satan is when men stand in need of advice how to kill Christ! The first word spoken by Pilate to Christ is his question: "Art Thou the king of the Jews?" This question clearly shows that, in this consultation of the Jews, they had agreed, as stated, to accuse the Lord Jesus before Pilate of desiring to excite sedition and to set Himself up for the king of the Jews. But what ground have they for such a charge? Where has Christ ever called Himself a king? Where has He attempted to pass Himself off as a lord? If they had been willing they might, on the other hand, have testified how He refused, departed and hid Himself, when the people attempted to take Him by force to make Him a king. They might have told too that He had commanded them not to keep back from Cæsar that which belonged to him, but to render to him his due. Now, we must also consider that Pilate could hardly have been satisfied with bare accusations, but must certainly have demanded proofs. And how were these furnished? No doubt, as follows. They had heard Christ confess to the chief priest that He was the Christ. Then they took the evidence of the Scriptures, showing from the Prophets how Christ should be a king. For Zechariah says: "Behold thy King cometh unto thee; He is just and having salvation, &c.;" and Hosea, in his 3. chapter, "They shall seek David their king;" and many other passages express the same. Therefore, since the Lord acknowledges Himself to be the Christ, He thereby acknowledges Himself to be also the king of the Jews. Behold, how accurate the researches of the devil!

But concerning that which goes against them and might serve the Lord Jesus, they are silent. Where Zechariah says: "Behold thy King cometh unto thee; He is just, and having salvation," he immediately adds, "lowly," that is, He shall be a spiritual King, who shall justify His own that believe in Him, and deliver them from death and all evil, that they might have consolation through Him against sin and God's wrath,—not a temporal king having business with money and possessions. He implies that God has ordained other kings who should control nations and individuals and possess opulence and power; but that these kings should not impart righteousness and salvation, which gifts are brought and bestowed alone by this King, of whom the Prophet says, "Behold thy King cometh," &c. These villains do not mention a syllable of this, but the naked idea that Christ had made Himself the king of the Jews is what they dress up for Pilate's sight. Thus Pilate, who would not have assisted them had their charge not exceeded what it was at first, viz., heresy and blasphemy, was beguiled into participating in their work.

Just so it goes to-day; for civil governments, at any rate, usually have the fault that they care very little for the kingdom of God and for religion. When kings and princes enjoy allegiance, tribute and royal glory, they are careless about everything else, and thus are satisfied that Pilate's throne should be the only one before which Christ appears. But the chief priests and elders of the people, i.e., the blood-thirsty mob composed of Pope, cardinal, bishops, monks and priests, come and accuse Christ before Pilate; they instigate the temporal authorities, such as emperors, kings and princes against the Gospel, as the Jews incited Pilate against Christ, saying that it teaches insurrection and that, unless its influence is checked in time, every subject will become a rebel. They urge the authorities to oppose the Gospel with zeal, if they would not have prosperity and happiness to forsake their scepter. Yea, these bloody, papal asses preach to the princes that it is the Gospel's fault that the Turk assails us and that we are not more successful in repelling him,—that the Gospel must be blamed for the great failures in our crops and for our being surrounded by misfortunes. By this means they arouse Pilate, who otherwise is not at all concerned about Christ and His preaching, to expose the Lord, and finally to command Him to be nailed to the cross.

Now, it cannot be helped that such falsehoods and virulent slander bring about painful results. But for this very reason have the Evangelists left us this history, so that, when like things come upon us, we may patiently bear them, saying, My Lord Jesus had to suffer the same. The servant is not better than his lord. Pilate would have permitted Christ to preach and perform miracles all His life, and would never have thought of interfering; but the high priests, the heartless horde, bring it to pass that Pilate as judge and Christ as criminal are brought together.

And so it is still; the Lord Jesus' greatest enemies are Pope, cardinal, bishops, monks and priests. When they have branded as heresy that which does not please them, or that which opposes them, they seek to hunt down the Gospel through worldly potentates; these latter must be their executioners and must, like Pilate, bedaub themselves with innocent blood, on the accusation and at the solicitation of these enemies. Pious Christian, bear it all! With thy Lord Jesus too they sported thus. Therefore, give thanks to God that thou art counted worthy to suffer for His name, as Luke tells us, in the 5. chapter of Acts, that the Apostles did! So much for the first part of our text.

The second part relates the terrible example of Judas. This the Evangelists so diligently portray that we may, as in à picture, recognize the peculiar character and nature of sin, and learn to shun it. For in Judas' case we see both how silently sin at first creeps in, but also how it afterwards causes such a horrible end.

We have heard, on a former occasion, what a seemingly small beginning this monstrous sin of Judas had, viz., that it began with his natural avarice and love of money. But its real fountain head we find in Judas' being such a godless hypocrite and such a wicked, desperate despiser of God. Thus, when the opportunity to make money out of the Lord Jesus presented itself, he regarded it a trifling matter to betray his innocent Lord and Master. Besides, he thinks it quite a prize that he can so soon possess himself of such an amount of money. At the Last Supper the Lord admonishes Judas so pointedly and so often, that he could not have misunderstood Him. But let the Lord preach to him and warn him ever so faithfully, it is all in vain; Judas does not lose sight of his object; his heart is riveted to the thirty pieces of silver! What a faithful, stern and earnest warning was not that which the Lord Jesus gave him, saying: "He that dippeth his hand with me in the dish, the same shall betray me;" again: "The Son of man goeth as it is written of Him; but woe unto that man by whom the Son of man is betrayed! It had been good for that man if he had not been born!" Should not Judas have taken these words to heart? Should he not have repented, saying: Great God, what have I not suffered the devil to put into my soul, miserable fellow that I am! But he does nothing of the kind; on the contrary, when he is so faithfully warned, he even asks whether his intentions are known. He puts the question: "Master, is it I?" The Lord answers him: "Thou hast said," i.e., yes, thou art he. But this matter, as already said, gave him no care nor trouble, because it was the means by which he could obtain so much money.

This should be remembered; for if we wish a correct picture of sin it must be painted as seeming at first sight an indifferent, simple thing, which is not at all dangerous. In committing sin men do not concern themselves about God's wrath; they fear no misfortune and they regard sin not as a burden, but as a little feather which a breath can balance in the air or drive away. Therefore, when sin assails us we do not fear it; yea, we rejoice in it and love it, and we even think that the more we can sin in doing our work, the better our work shall be done. Suppose we illustrate this by the case of an avaricious usurer, an adulterer or a drunkard. Upon such Paul passes an appalling judgment, when he says, 1 Cor. 6: "Be not deceived; neither fornicators, nor idolaters, nor adulterers, nor covetous, nor drunkards shall inherit the kingdom of God." This terrible decree is written here, is preached too, and the very ones who are subject to such vices get to hear it; but they accept it no more than Judas accepted it. Could they only dispose of their property so as to make it yield them twenty or thirty per cent; could only their evil desires be satisfied; could they only have gay companions every day and be jolly and drunk every night,—then would they think themselves very fortunate and, neither caring for nor grieving over the judgment pronounced upon them, be in good spirits and perfectly merry.

This is spoken for the common people who grossly tread in Judas' footsteps. But exceedingly dreadful it is that to-day the Pope and his minions persecute and condemn God's Word, the acknowledged truth, invent many base and blasphemous lies against this Word, and induce worldly potentates to use their power against it and to exterminate the truth of God and all who hold it, so that Judas' trade may be made to flourish as formerly. And then they are so utterly blind and obdurate that their conscience does not trouble them, and that they think it would be an excellent thing to overflow this land with blood. What blindness,—what diabolical enmity against Christ's Word and the true Church! But more of this hereafter.

Adam preached the same thing to Cain, his son, and warned him against sin, when he perceived what hatred there was in his heart toward his brother Abel. He says to him, Gen. 4: "If thou doest well, shalt thou not be accepted? and if thou doest not well, sin lieth at the door." By this he meant to say: Make thyself well acquainted with sin; for when it attacks a man it always is as a wild, rapacious beast, which pretends to be asleep and lets men handle and stroke it; no one fears and no one is hurt. Even as innocent as this does sin seem. It is a smooth, pretty kitten, which permits itself to be played with and caressed. But be careful, saith Adam; it sleeps, indeed, but will not sleep forever. Why not? Because it "lieth at the door," in a public place, where every one comes and goes; nothing easier, therefore, than that it should awake. And then it will be a furious lion, an angry bear, tearing to pieces and destroying all in its way. Now, as Adam had foretold to Cain, so it came. Adam commanded him to conquer sin, and not let sin rule and lead him. But Cain gave no heed; he let sin have its own way; he slew his brother. Sin did not rest long here; its sleep was soon over, and then it tortured Cain until he did not know where to stay. He dared not remain with his father and mother, and besides, had fears for his body and his life.

Let us mark well this second characteristic of sin! At first it sleeps and seems a trifling, harmless thing. But it sleeps not long, and when it awakes it becomes a grievous burden which we cannot bear without God's special help. This we see in the case of the traitor Judas. While sin rested, it was impossible for him to fear; the glossy fur deceived him so, that he did not perceive the sharp, poisonous claws. But its rest could not last a great while, for it lay at the door where it could be easily waked. Where all pleading and all admonition failed before, now a single moment comes and drives such terror to his soul that he knows not what to do. For when he sees the Lord led to Pilate he fears that the Lord's life is imperiled, is sorry, and now perceives, for the first time, what he has done. Now sin awakes and, according to its natural way, acts with such fury and horror that he cannot bear it. Before, he so loved the thirty pieces of silver that, for the sake of having them, he could betray and sell the Lord Jesus without a pang; now, the matter stands reversed. If he now had the money and wealth of all the world, he would give it all to save the Lord Jesus' life. Since it was love of money that made him so miserable, and his purpose to possess it that brought this sin upon him, he now hates money so, that he has neither rest nor peace in its possession, but runs after the high priests into the temple, confesses that he has done wrong, and offers to give them back the money if they will only liberate Jesus. And when the chief priests will not do this, to get rid of the money at all events he casts it down at their feet. Now, this is the peculiar character of sin; when it awakes it so violently attacks conscience and preaches a sermon of such horrors that the frightened heart knows not what to do and what not to do. And sin inflicts the further calamity, that, as little as is the consolation which the poor creature finds in himself, so little too is the comfort he derives from others. Judas honestly tells the chief priests his troubles. Alas, he says, "I have sinned,—I have betrayed the innocent blood!" But how do they console him? "What is that to us? see thou to that," they tell him. They shove everything over to the shoulders of Judas, and let the intolerable load lie there, unwilling in the least to help the poor, frightened soul with words of consolation or of counsel.

Now follows the third and last calamity. For when it so happens that sin persists in castigating conscience, the devil does not loiter, but pokes and blows the fire until the red flames rage within, and all attempts at rescue seem vain. In such fear and agony Judas is urged on by Satan until he goes out quickly, and in his misery hangs himself. Now, this is the end which Satan from the beginning sought to bring about by sin. He who could, at the beginning, consider and credit this end, would surely pray and guard against it. But it is hidden; sin is very quiet, and does not disclose in the start what its final object is. So much for the history of poor, unhappy Judas, who for a trifle sold the Lord Jesus, and who not only did not enjoy this money, but also lost on its account body, life, soul and salvation.

Therefore, study well this example, and let its memory nevermore depart; for it is to help me and you and all of us to an accurate knowledge of sin, and to serve us as a shield against it. If we do not mark this example and learn from it to know sin, we are liable to be deceived by sin and are exposed to the damage which it does. For, in the first place, it is the nature of sin so to flatter and please the old Adam that he delights in it and loves it; but this lasts only until sin awakes. Then, in the second place, follow trouble, toil, fear, danger, terrors, tremblings, despair and, finally, eternal death. Let us recognize these two features of sin from the case of Judas, and not suffer ourselves to be deluded like the world, which accepts neither instruction nor reproof, being deceived by sin's beautiful, fair and cheerful countenance! Many a citizen, peasant and nobleman knows how to make an easy living. If he has anything for sale, he tries to get the highest price. When he buys, he tries to buy as cheap as possible. He is not content with what his houses have brought him hitherto, but raises the rent. And When he disposes of money, wheat or other commodities, he has an eye to his best interests. Such a course soothes and pleases our Adam's nature. Every one thinks his shrewdness to have been admirable when he, by some means or other, has obtained and laid by in one year, say one, two or three hundred dollars, according to the nature of his business. Hence we see every one pursuing his daily bread, and this with all manner of haste.

This is the very sin of which Judas was guilty in the beginning of his career. The world to-day does just as Judas did; it does not fear this sin and thinks there is no danger in it. But why? Simply because sin rests and sleeps and rarely shows its nature in the start. Sin paints and adorns itself; it puts on the mask of beauty and of youth; in this way it hides its hideousness. But if we could at once unmask it and wash off its paint with strong lye, we would run away from it as from the devil. No one would consent to extortion and addict himself to avarice, if he knew what the consequence will be when sin begins to rack the conscience and when remorse comes. For the numerous examples which we have, prove that people who pursue only money and possessions, cannot in the last hour abandon their accustomed course of thought. In that hour their hearts are closed to all consolation from God's Word, for their thoughts are even then rambling through the counting-room, the market and the warehouse, and engaged with this or that debt not yet collected. In short, thorns have so enclosed them that they cannot flee; or else their consciences are so molested as to make them totally unfit for taking comfort.

What has been said applies not only to the bag of Judas, i.e., avarice, but to all sins. For, no matter where it sleeps, sin finally must awake, and it always then creates such wretchedness as was that of Judas. Still, this is done especially in the true disciples of Judas, who, for the sake of money and possessions, oppose the Word of God, persecute the Gospel, and give occasion for false doctrine and idolatry. Such disciples are the Pope, his cardinals, bishops, worthless lords, priests, monks, doctors and the like, who crowd around Judas' bag and fight for it. No wonder, for this bag is not prickly and thorny, but its touch is very soft and velvety; in other words, the world loudly applauds those who have succeeded in securing sufficient means for living at ease and in splendor. Besides, it seems a trifle to violate the Word of God in this respect or that, thus sinning against the acknowledged truth, and to act contrary to one's convictions; yea, it seems an easy thing for the prebendary who occupies the cathedral, and for the minister who moderates himself, to justify their unwillingness to speak the truth openly. For the world and the devil pay big wages for such work. But when sin awakes, the little, black, rabid dog, Remorse, will surely come, and touch and terrify thy conscience so, that thou shalt find consolation nowhere, and thus be hurled into despair by the machinations of the devil. Then shalt thou have received the same reward with Judas.

It were well, therefore, to consider this danger in time, to forego bishoprics, canonries, Epicureanism and the like, to resolve to be a Christian, to further and confess God's Word, and to walk before God with a clear conscience. Even if we had no superabundance of bread, God would still give us our daily bread and not suffer us to starve, for He says: "Seek ye first the kingdom of God, and all these things shall be added unto you."

The following, therefore, is what this history teaches. Since sin, at first, is quiet and sleeps, but afterward awakes and fills conscience with all misery, by which Satan then drives his victims into despair, we should beware of sin, do nothing against our better knowledge and, besides, ask God daily, yea, every moment, for His Holy Spirit, that He may not lead us into temptation, but mercifully save us from falling and shield us from sin. It has already been stated that we are not apprehensive of the evil results of sin, because sin is not awake in the beginning, but sleeps, and that deception and ruin, therefore, are very near us. For this reason we ought to pray without ceasing, and be very careful everywhere, so that sin may not steal upon us unawares.

But when the fall has occurred and we have been deceived, and when sin, which slept at first, now awakes, appears to us and upbraids us, we must be prepared for this encounter, and from the example of Judas we can learn how to be prepared. For how clearly do we not see what was the matter with Judas! Satan converted his sin into a mountain so huge and lofty that it shut out from his sight God, together with His Word, His promises and His mercy; hence, he simply despairs. Now, when we trace this confusion back to its origin, can we deny that Judas could have consoled himself even in such great distress, had he not set at naught God's Word, but more eagerly studied and obeyed it? Having always despised and neglected the Word, is it to be wondered at that now, when he stands in need of its comfort and aid he must do without them? Therefore, as we must, on the one hand, guard ourselves, with godliness and constant prayer, against sleeping sin, so that we may not be deceived and seduced; so also, on the other hand, when sin awakes, and chastises and disturbs us, we must defend and support ourselves with the Holy Gospel. This Gospel shows us Christ as Him who suffered and made satisfaction for the sins of the whole world. And in this Gospel we find that God, the Almighty Creator and Father, desires not the death of a sinner; but that He does desire the sinner to return and live, that is, to acknowledge and lament his sins and to hope for forgiveness through the Lord Jesus. But Judas had not these Gospel gifts; hence he despaired.

Again, Peter also fell shamefully, and experienced such pangs as those of Judas. Sin slept at first; in other words, his denying Christ did not seem specially dangerous to Peter; but it finally awakes and so torments his heart that he cannot sufficiently bewail his fall, or, as the Evangelists have it, "He went out and wept bitterly." But why is it that Peter does not hang himself like Judas? Simply because Peter, no doubt, remembered the Word of the Lord Jesus; this saved him. He must have remembered that the Lord had prophesied to him that he should fall, and also that He had comforted him, saying, as we read Luke 22., "Simon, Simon, behold, Satan hath desired to have you, that he may sift you as wheat: but I have prayed for thee, that thy faith fail not: and when thou art converted, strengthen thy brethren."

This sermon Peter heard and kept. This Word was the staff that supported him; sin could not now crush him to earth; had it been otherwise, sin would have done with him as it did with Judas. God's Word saved him. O, learn this well, and thus be prepared for like emergencies; hear God's Word frequently; never go to bed and never rise from sleep without repeating one, two, three or four of its beautiful passages!

Christ says, Matt. 9: "I am not come to call the righteous, but sinners to repentance." Matt. 11: "Come unto me, all ye that labor and are heavy laden, and I will give you rest. Take my yoke upon you, and learn of me; for I am meek and lowly in heart: and ye shall find rest unto your souls. For my yoke is easy, and my burden is light." Jno. 3: "For God so loved the world, that He gave His only begotten Son, that whosoever believeth in Him should not perish, but have everlasting life. For God sent not His Son into the world to condemn the world; but that the world through Him might be saved. He that believeth on Him is not condemned." Again, Jno. 3: "The Father loveth the Son, and hath given all things into His hand. He that believeth on the Son hath everlasting life: and he that believeth not the Son shall not see life: but the wrath of God abideth on him." Jno. 5: "Verily, verily, I say unto you, he that heareth my word and believeth on Him that sent me, hath everlasting life, and shall not come into condemnation, but is passed from death unto life." Jno. 11: "I am the resurrection, and the life: he that believeth on me, though he were dead, yet shall he live." 1 Jno. 2: "If any man sin, we have an advocate with the Father, Jesus Christ the righteous: and He is the propitiation for our sins: and not for ours only, but also for the sins of the whole world." If we daily practice such and similar passages, and by practicing familiarize ourselves with them, we then possess the infallible remedy for all spiritual ailments. But unhappy Judas had not this remedy at hand.

We have more such examples. Dreadful was the fall of David; his was a more heinous sin than were the sins which king Saul committed in the beginning of his apostasy. How, then, are we to account for it that Saul cuts his throat, while David finds deliverance? Saul had not God's Word; therefore, when sin raged and reproached him, he could not defend himself; for he had nothing on which to lay hold. Sin, when it awaked, reproached David also, and with such severity that he himself pronounced his judgment, saying, that he had deserved to die. But in this time of need he holds to the word of the prophet Nathan, who tells him that God is gracious, and that He will not impute to him his sin. Let us, then, learn well this second lesson taught us here, viz., not only to shun sin, but also, when sin awakes, to be able to contend with it and to protect ourselves. But during our whole life we must prepare for such distress, equipping ourselves with the Word of God, else we shall have no aid nor counsel, as Judas' case shows plainly. How Judas rejoiced at first over the thirty pieces of silver! They were in his sight as a meadow mown, for sin rested not. But when sin awoke, these thirty pieces of silver became a burden which he could not bear, and so, to relieve his conscience of this load, he hanged himself. All he effected by this means, however, was, that he had to bear the burden in eternity. Of such an end beware; do not let sin creep in; live in the fear of God; keep conscience clear, and attentively hear God's Word: then consolation shall be thine in need of every kind!

The Evangelists further relate that the chief priests took counsel about the thirty pieces of silver. They would not put them into the treasury, but bought with them the potter's field, of which they made a burial-place for strangers. The prophecy, of which this was the fulfillment, does not appear remarkable. However, since the Evangelist takes the pains to quote that which the prophet Zechariah had predicted long before, the prophecy cannot be meaningless, but must have its peculiar signification. The following is, no doubt, its proper explanation.

The citizens of Jerusalem had their cemeteries, while strangers, as we see here, had none. Now, in the true Jerusalem, the Christian Church, we find that the Jews, according to the 147. Psalm, are God's people: "He showeth His Word unto Jacob." But to us Gentiles, who are strangers, the kingdom of God does not belong; for the same Psalm continues to sing: "He hath not dealt so with any nation," &c. But the thirty pieces of silver, for which our dear Lord Jesus was sold, have bought a burial-place for us pilgrims too; that is, the innocent sufferings and death of Christ have blessed us Gentiles also with the hope of everlasting life. For the Lord had to bleed and die in consequence of being sold for thirty pieces of silver. Therefore, the Evangelist teaches us from the Prophets that we should not forget for whom the Lord was sold, for whom He suffered, and for whom He died. It was not alone for His people, to whom He had been promised, but also for us Gentiles, who before had no final resting-place in the true Jerusalem. Those thirty pieces of silver, which Judas received for Christ, have bought us a share in the acre of our God. Now we shall be laid into that glorious grave, bed-chamber magnificent, from which our Lord Jesus will call us forth on the judgment-day, when He shall also give us everlasting joy. May our dear Father in heaven grant us this through His Holy Spirit. Amen.

7

Christc Accused before Pilate and Condemned to Death

Meanwhile Jesus stood before the governor, and the governor asked him, "Are you the king of the Jews?" "You have said so," Jesus replied. When he was accused by the chief priests and the elders, he gave no answer. Then Pilate asked him, "Don't you hear the testimony they are bringing against you?" But Jesus made no reply, not even to a single charge—to the great amazement of the governor. Now it was the governor's custom at the festival to release a prisoner chosen by the crowd. At that time they had a well-known prisoner whose name was Jesus Barabbas. So when the crowd had gathered, Pilate asked them, "Which one do you want me to release to you: Jesus Barabbas, or Jesus who is called the Messiah?" For he knew it was out of self-interest that they had handed Jesus over to him. While Pilate was sitting on the judge's seat, his wife sent him this message: "Don't have anything to do with that innocent man, for I have suffered a great deal today in a dream because of him." But the chief priests and the elders persuaded the crowd to ask for Barabbas and to have Jesus executed. "Which of the two do you want me to release to you?" asked the governor. "Barabbas," they answered. "What shall I do, then, with Jesus who is called the Messiah?" Pilate asked. They all answered, "Crucify him!" "Why? What crime has he committed?" asked Pilate. But they shouted all the louder, "Crucify him!" When Pilate saw that he was getting nowhere, but that instead an uproar was starting, he took water and washed his hands in front of the crowd. "I am innocent of this man's blood," he said. "It is your responsibility!" All the people answered, "His blood is on us and on our children!" Then he released Barabbas to them. But he had Jesus flogged, and handed him over to be crucified.

—MATTHEW 27:11–31.

In a recent sermon you heard, dear friends, how the Lord Jesus was tried before the chief priest. We are now ready to learn what happened Him after He was delivered to Pilate. Each Evangelist has his own way of relating these things and does not go into all the details, but one states this, another that, for which reason it is necessary to compile the items stated by each, and then to relate these items in their historical order.

The first item is furnished by the Evangelist John, who says that when, early in the morning, they led Jesus from the palace of Caiaphas unto the hall of judgment, they themselves went not in, lest they should be defiled and become disqualified to eat the passover. Since they were required to separate themselves from those as unclean who accidentally entered a house in which some one had died, they concluded that it might defile them to go into the judgment hall, in which the sentence of death was pronounced. It did not occur to these blind people that it was a far greater sin to shed innocent blood. Such holiness prevails among our Papists too, who think that eating flesh on Friday or eggs in the passion-week is a much greater sin than to persecute and strangle poor Christians for the Gospel's sake. They go about the latter with hearts as light as though it were a trifle. But about the former, which is no sin at all, but merely a human prohibition, they are exceedingly conscientious. Since these holy people refuse to go into the hall of judgment, Pilate was constrained to go out to them. He asked them: "What accusation bring ye against this man?" Impudently and with arrogance they reply: "If He were not a male factor, we would not have delivered Him up unto thee." Just as if they were so upright and pious that we should not suppose them capable of undertaking anything wrong! But Pilate meets them nobly when he says: "Take ye Him, and judge Him according to your law." This was as much as saying: It is not customary with us Romans to judge a man without first trying him; but if you Jews think it is right to do so, why, you may take and kill Him, but I will not. Thus we clearly see that the Jews, after they had taken all necessary counsel, still have no confidence in themselves; they fear that their accusation will not stand the test. Nevertheless, they are unwilling to accept Pilate's decision without a reply, for it stung them to the quick, and therefore they answer: "It is not lawful for us to put any man to death." This meant: If we had the authority to do this, we should not have called on you; but the Emperor has taken criminal jurisdiction away from us and confided it to you; therefore, act according to your office.

John adds here: "That the saying of Jesus might be fulfilled, which He spake, signifying what death He should die." For, as we read Matthew 20. and Luke 17., Christ had foretold to His disciples that He should be delivered to the Gentiles. For the sake, however, of having a charge to make, they accused Him, as Luke writes, in these words: "We found this fellow perverting the nation, and forbidding to give tribute to Cæsar, saying that He Himself is Christ a king." Here we hear why they delivered Him to Pilate. But the account sufficiently shows how basely they belie our dear Lord. Christ could, indeed, have strongly confuted them by referring them to His words: "Render therefore unto Cæsar the things which are Cæsar's, and unto God the things that are God's;" but what good would it have done? He had to suffer Himself to be accused of being a rebel, of turning the nation away from the Emperor, of forbidding the paying of tribute, and of desiring to be a king.

Just so, at this day, the Pope, cardinals, bishops, monks and priests calumniate the holy Gospel, charging it with teaching sedition, and saying that unless it is opposed the temporal power will come into disrepute and no one will respect it. But let this not offend thee; thank God that thou knowest that they, the desperate miscreants, most invidious foes of the Lord Jesus and most malignant blasphemers of Christ's Gospel, lie! For the Gospel deals with other and loftier things: it teaches how we can be freed from sin and attain to eternal life, alone by believing in the Son of God. This is the character of the instructions given us by the Gospel; it does not meddle with worldly things, leaves these so to remain as God has already disposed of them by means of the temporal government, and exhorts to obedience to this government.

When Pilate now had heard the accusation, he was in no haste to act upon it, but, as John says, entered into the judgment hall again, ordered Jesus to be brought before him and asked Him, saying: "Art Thou the king of the Jews?" Jesus answered him: "Sayest thou this thing of thyself, or did others tell it thee of me?" As though He would say: O, if my enemies would acquit me, you would soon do so too; for I know that you do not regard me as a king nor as one who would be likely to make an uproar.

"Pilate answered: Am I a Jew? Thine own nation and the chief priests have delivered Thee unto me; what hast Thou done? Jesus answered, My kingdom is not of this world; if my kingdom were of this world, then would my servants fight, that I should not be delivered to the Jews; but now is my kingdom not from hence. Pilate therefore said unto Him, Art Thou a king then? Jesus answered, Thou sayest that I am a king. To this end was I born, and for this cause came I into the world, that I should bear witness unto the truth. Every one that is of the truth heareth my voice. Pilate saith unto Him, what is truth?" As if he would say: If Thou art a king sent to bear witness unto the truth, we have no reason to fear Thee; for, with this as Thy object, Thou wilt not injure the Emperor. The proud Gentile meant to say, in other words: Truth is not the cause of a great deal of strife. And this is only too true, and especially in these evil and latter days does truth go begging. It is deceitfulness, fraud, avarice, usury and the like that elevate a man in these times. But what is gained by these in the end will soon be seen.

When Pilate had sufficiently examined the Lord, he went out again unto the Jews and said: "I find in Him no fault at all,"—"I have found no fault in this man." But the Jews, as Luke relates, "were the more fierce, saying, He stirreth up the people, teaching throughout all Jewry, beginning from Galilee to this place. When Pilate heard of Galilee, he asked whether the man were a Galilean. And as soon as he knew that He belonged unto Herod's jurisdiction, he sent Him to Herod, who himself also was at Jerusalem at that time. And when Herod saw Jesus, he was exceeding glad; for he was desirous to see Him of a long season, because he had heard many things of Him; and he hoped to have seen some miracle done by Him. Then he questioned with Him in many words; but He answered him nothing. And the chief priests and scribes stood and vehemently accused Him. And Herod with his men of war set Him at naught, and mocked Him, and arrayed Him in a gorgeous robe, and sent Him again to Pilate. And the same day Pilate and Herod were made friends together; for before they were at enmity between themselves."

Here some might wonder why the Lord converses so with Pilate, giving him all information, but refuses to speak one word with Herod, who, besides, was king of Galilee. The true reason for this we find in

Herod's being a totally abandoned scoundrel and, at the same time, a great hypocrite. He had lately caused John the Baptist to be beheaded, and lived a life of public scandal by having his brother Philip's wife, and still pretended to be exceedingly pious. For this reason the Lord, in the Gospel, calls him a fox,—an animal of which the fur is the only valuable part,—a ravenous, but still a very cunning animal. Such people are not worthy of intercourse with others; they are hypocrites who adopt holy faces and gentle speech, as it is written of Herod in Mark 6., where it says that he "feared John, knowing that he was a just man and a holy; ... and when he heard him, he did many things, and heard him gladly." But such people are not in earnest. Scoffers they are, who regard the Gospel as a fable, and who look upon the Christian as a great fool for offending great lords and endangering his possessions by his faith. Let everyone, therefore, avoid such people, and do as Christ here did with Herod, have no communication with them.

This also is worthy of observation here that just as Pilate and Herod, who before were enemies, now become friends by their contact with Christ the Lord, even so do we see men act in our day. Men who could not be reconciled among themselves before, are harmonious in their opposition to the Gospel. One bishop cannot agree with another, and one order cannot be friendly toward another order. Princes are dissatisfied with each other. Each one wishes to be the best, to have the preference, and to oppress and silence all the rest. But when Christ comes among them and His Gospel shows its might, they all unite, are the best friends in the world, and stand together with their goods and lives, as David prophesied long ago in the 2. Psalm.

After the Lord was brought again from Herod to Pilate, "Pilate," so says Luke, "when he had called together the chief priests and the rulers and the people, said unto them, Ye have brought this man unto me, as one that perverteth the people; and behold, I, having examined Him before you, have found no fault in this man touching those things whereof ye accuse Him; no, nor yet Herod; for I sent you to him; and lo, nothing worthy of death is done unto Him. I will therefore chastise Him and release Him. (For of necessity he must release one unto them at the feast.)"

"And they had then," says Matthew, as we have heard, "a notable prisoner, called Barabbas." Him Pilate places before the Jews, together with

Christ, that the Jews might choose between the two, hoping that no one would ask for Barabbas, as he was a great rebel and murderer, well worthy of death.

"But the chief priests and elders persuaded the multitude that they should ask Barabbas." "And," so Luke proceeds, "they cried out all at once, saying, Away with this man and release unto us Barabbas; (who for a certain sedition made in the city, and for murder, was cast into prison.) Pilate, therefore, willing to release Jesus, spake again to them. But they cried, saying, Crucify Him, crucify Him. And he said unto them the third time, Why, what evil hath He done? I have found no cause of death in Him; I will therefore chastise Him, and let Him go. And they were instant with loud voices, requiring that He might be crucified."

Matthew writes that when Pilate "was set down on the judgment seat, his wife sent unto him, saying, Have thou nothing to do with that just man; for I have suffered many things this day in a dream because of Him."

And this was, indeed, an excellent warning, sent perhaps by some good angel, who, in a dream, announced to Pilate's wife the misfortunes and calamities which Pilate would bring upon himself and his house in case he should listen to the Jews and, at their command, destroy the innocent Jesus. But as admonitions were useless and vain in Judas' case, so did they at last avail nothing with Pilate. Nevertheless, he resists the Jews for a while. The Jews, to whom Christ was promised, wish the most villainous murderer to live, but Him, the Prince of life, they are in haste to slay. Since in this way Pilate's proposition to "let Him go" is discouraged, Pilate makes still another effort: he takes Jesus and scourges Him, as the Evangelists continue to relate.

"Then the soldiers of the governor took Jesus into the common hall, and gathered unto Him the whole band of soldiers. And they stripped Him," "and scourged Him," "and put on Him a scarlet robe. And when they had platted a crown of thorns, they put it upon His head, and a reed in His right hand" instead of a scepter; "and they bowed the knee before Him, and mocked Him," "and began to salute Him," "saying, Hail, King of the Jews!" and smote Him in the face. "And they spit upon Him, and took the reed, and smote Him on the head," "and bowing their knees worshiped Him."

Here and throughout the entire Passion-history you will observe, dear Christian, how Satan poured out all his poisonous, bitter, hellish hatred, rage and fury upon our dear Lord in such a way that surely no human being ever has endured such great and dreadful suffering, torture, insult, abuse and derision as the Son of God; and this He bore for the sake of my sin, thy sin and the sin of all the world. But now, since the suffering and death of Christ are the only sacrifice that was able to expiate sin, it is easy to calculate how immensely great and terrible God's wrath against sin must be; and also, how ineffably, yea, unfathomably great must be His grace and mercy toward us condemned beings,—that grace and mercy whereby He gave His only begotten Son to die an ignominious death upon the cross for our sins.

Now it was customary among the Romans to beat malefactors before executing them; for which reason Pilate commanded Christ also to be scourged. At the same time he still hopes and labors to liberate the Lord. Therefore he led Jesus forth, after the soldiers had scourged Him and put on Him the purple robe and the crown of thorns, and said to the Jews: "Behold, I bring Him forth to you, that ye may know that I find no fault in Him."

"Then," says John, "came Jesus forth, wearing the crown of thorns, and the purple robe. And Pilate saith unto them, Behold the man!" meaning by this: You should be satisfied with such punishment as this, seeing that your accusations are so groundless and His innocence is so evident. But neither did he succeed in this way.

As soon as the chief priests and their officers saw Jesus, and perceived that Pilate still sought to acquit Him, "they cried out, saying, Crucify Him, crucify Him." Pilate was displeased with such great injustice, "for," as we are informed by Matthew, "he knew that for envy they had delivered Him." Therefore he answers them bluntly: "Take ye Him and crucify Him; for I find no fault in Him. The Jews answered him, We have a law, and by our law He ought to die, because He made Himself the Son of God."

"When Pilate therefore heard that saying, he was the more afraid; and went again into the judgment hall, and saith unto Jesus, Whence art Thou? But Jesus gave him no answer. Then saith Pilate unto Him, Speakest Thou not unto me? knowest Thou not that I have power to crucify Thee, and have power to release Thee? Jesus answered, Thou couldest have no power at all against me, except it were given thee from above; therefore he that delivered me unto thee hath the greater sin."

And this was also a powerful warning. For Pilate here went too far, thinking that in virtue of his authority Jesus' fate was in his hands, to be decided for or against Him at his own pleasure, as temporal authorities in such pride commit many sins. No, Pilate, says Christ, you overdo this matter; keep within proper bounds. If you have power, you have it not of yourself; power comes from above. Therefore, use your power in such a manner that you may know how to give an account of its exercise. Pilate accepts this admonition, and seeks the more how he might release Him. But the Jews would not hear of such a thing and "cried out, saying, If thou let this man go, thou art not Cæsar's friend; whosoever maketh himself a king speaketh against Cæsar."

"When Pilate therefore heard that saying, he brought Jesus forth, and sat down in the judgment seat in a place that is called the Pavement, but in the Hebrew, Gabbatha. And it was the preparation of the passover, and about the sixth hour," i.e., about noon. "And he saith unto the Jews, Behold your King!" in other words, You still maintain that He had made Himself a king. Alas, for the king! You do Him great injustice. Does He look like a king or like a seditious person? But all was vain; "They cried out, Away with Him, away with Him, crucify Him! Pilate saith unto them, Shall I crucify your King? The chief priests answered, We have no king but Cæsar."

"When Pilate saw that he could prevail nothing, but that rather a tumult was made," he was "willing to content the people" and "gave sentence that it should be as they required," and "took water, and washed his hands before the multitude, saying, I am innocent of the blood of this just person; see ye to it. Then answered all the people, and said, His blood be on us, and on our children;" that is, if we do Him wrong, then may we and our children be punished for it. "Then released he Barabbas unto them,"—"him that for sedition and murder was cast into prison, whom they had desired; but he delivered Jesus," mocked and scourged, "to their will," "to be crucified." These are the things that happened the Lord Jesus before Pilate.

8

Explanation of Several Points in the History just Given

This part of the history of our Lord Jesus furnishes us with many excellent points of Christian doctrine, laden with consolation. Since, however, the material presented here is too much for one sermon, and the narrative itself is sufficiently lengthy, we shall dwell only on three points. The first is this: Pilate and others frequently testify to the innocence of our dear Lord Jesus. The second: Christ witnessed a good confession before Pilate,—which is also highly extolled by St. Paul, 1 Tim. 6. The third: Both Pilate and the Jews treat the blood of the Lord as a trifle, but it afterward becomes an intolerable and everlasting burden, which sinks them into temporal and eternal misery.

With reference to the first point, you must have noticed throughout that Pilate always insists upon it that he finds no cause of death in Christ. His wife also sent unto him, telling him to have nothing to do with that just and innocent man. Pilate moreover discovers, from all the actions of the Jews and by diligent investigation, that the chief priests and elders were moved against Christ by nothing but malice and envy. Similar testimony, but in greater measure and more powerful, was borne after the death of Christ. Great and glorious miracles then were wrought. The sun lost his lustre and deep darkness reigned, the vail of the temple was rent in twain, the earth did quake, the rocks rent, the graves were opened, and many bodies of the saints arose. Then the centurion openly confessed: "Certainly this was a righteous man." And all the people present, beholding and taking to heart the things which were done, smote their breasts, to signify that the rash execution of the dear, innocent Lord gave them pain.

But of what use is this testimony? Why do the Evangelists so carefully relate it? Without a doubt, their only object is to point us to the counsel and will of God, and to admonish us to consider why the Lord, being innocent and just, had to suffer so. In other words, they wish, in view of the abundant proof that Christ was innocent and did not deserve to die, to make us firmer in our faith. They desire to convince us that whatever our blessed Lord Jesus suffered, He suffered for us; and that God laid these afflictions upon Him, and, although He was innocent, would not remove them, so that, by His bearing them, sin might be removed from us and we might be reconciled again to God.

Whenever, therefore, we read in any part of the Passion history how unjustly the Jews and Gentiles treated the Lord Jesus, how they smote Him before the high priest, set Him at naught before Herod, and mocked and scourged Him in the judgment hall,—whenever, I say, we hear of such treatment, no matter where it is recorded, our thoughts must run thus: Behold, He is innocent; He does not bear this for Himself; He has not merited this. But I and you and all of us have deserved this suffering; death and every misfortune did rest upon us because of sin; but here the innocent and holy Son of God appears, takes upon Himself my debts, thy debts, and the debts of all of us, and discharges them, so that we might be free. When these are our thoughts we shall have such comfort that our hearts cannot despair on account of their sin, and that we shall not flee from God as though He were a tyrant or an executioner; but that we shall turn unto Him with heart-felt confidence and praise and glorify His mercy, which, as Paul says in the 5. chap, of Romans, He commendeth toward us in that He delivered His only begotten Son, our Lord and Savior, unto death, to die for us sinners. Who could or would doubt that God's intentions toward us are good and altogether gracious?

Sin had subjected all of us to the wrath of God and to death, and had transferred us into Satan's kingdom; eternal life was lost, and in its place had been inherited every calamity for time and for eternity. But our Father, merciful and gracious, comes to our relief, and, rather than permit us to remain in such misery, sends His only begotten Son, born of a virgin and made under the law, so that the law, although flesh and blood were unable to do God's will, might not have been given in vain, but might be fulfilled by this Man for all other men. And finally God suffers Him to die upon the cross, by His innocent death to atone for our sins, so that we, being released from eternal death and from the kingdom of Satan, might receive eternal life and be the children of God.

Believing that this was done on thy account and for thy welfare, take it as thine own and let it comfort thee. And well may we do this; for here we hear not once, not twice, but many times, that all that Jesus suffers He suffers innocently. But why does God tolerate this, yea, why does He ordain and bring it about? Simply that thou mightest be comforted in Christ. He does not suffer for Himself, but for thee and for all mankind, even as John says: "He is the propitiation for our sins: and not for ours only, but also for the sins of the whole world." For this reason John the Baptist calls Him "The Lamb of God, which taketh away the sin of the world," that is, a divinely appointed Sacrifice, who takes the sin of all the world upon Himself, so that this sin may rest upon the world no longer. This accounts for the seeming inconsistency. He is the Son of God, perfectly holy and altogether without sin, and therefore it were but just that He should not be subject to the curse and to death. We are sinners and under the curse and wrath of God, and therefore it were but just that we should suffer death and damnation. But God has reversed this relation; He who knows no sin, who is altogether merciful, and in whom, as John says, dwells the fullness of God's grace, was made a curse for us and had to bear sin's punishment, while we, through Him, have obtained mercy and have become the children of God. We should, therefore, cling to this consolation and take special delight in such testimony for Christ's innocence. For what Christ innocently suffered was caused by our sins. Therefore His innocence comforts us against all sin and suffering; for His innocence is a sure and lasting evidence that His passion is for our benefit, and that our dear Lord and merciful Redeemer has suffered for us and paid our debts. However, since we shall have occasion to speak further of this when we come to Christ's crucifixion between the murderers, we shall now proceed to the second point.

St. Paul, 1 Tim. 6., admonishes Timothy thus: "I give thee charge in the sight of God, who quickeneth all things, and before Christ Jesus, who before Pontius Pilate witnessed a good confession, that thou keep this commandment," that is, doctrine, "without spot, unrebukable, until the appearing of our Lord Jesus Christ."

Because this passage mentions so directly the confession which our dear Lord Jesus made before Pilate, and Paul makes use of it for earnestly admonishing Timothy, we have reason to meditate upon this confession and to inquire what it is and what is its purpose. Now, the Gospels tell us plainly what it was that Christ confessed. When the Jews had accused Him of having said that He was a king, and Pilate had taken Him to task on this account, He did not deny, but confessed openly before Pilate: "My kingdom is not of this world," i.e., my kingdom is no corporeal, earthly kingdom. Then Pilate asked again, "Art Thou a king then? Jesus answered, Thou sayest that I am a king. To this end was I born, and for this cause came I into the world, that I should bear witness unto the truth. Every one that is of the truth heareth my voice." Do you ask: But of what use was this confession to Paul in admonishing Timothy to keep the commandment, i.e. doctrine, pure and not to adulterate it? Truly, of much use! Everything, if we desire to be true ministers and Christians, depends upon our believing what Christ confessed, viz.: that He is a king; but that His kingdom is not of this world; that His only work in this world is to bear witness unto the truth. And it follows that His earthly subjects must be like Him, the King. He is indeed called a king; but when He is compared with Herod, Pilate and other temporal kings and rulers, he seems a poor, wretched man. Herod was a great, shining lord, who courted sensual delight, realized his heart's desires, and was looked upon by all the world as glorious. So the world regarded Pilate too and others. But poor, innocent Christ bears no comparison with such as they; yea, men mock and scorn Him as they please; they nail Him to the cross and murder Him. Therefore He said: "My kingdom is not of this world!"

Why, then, is He called a king? Because He is a king,—a king "just, and having salvation," as Zechariah says, chapter 9. Therefore, whosoever lives in His kingdom must not expect Him to give money or possessions, to satisfy the body's wants, or to do the other things which earthly kings are wont to do. No, this King forgives sins; He bestows righteousness; He delivers from everlasting death; He bestows the Holy Spirit and eternal life. These are His gifts to all who hear His voice. This kingdom He has established on earth, but only in the Word and in faith.

We have, therefore, an eternal King omnipotent, Christ Jesus, God's own Son, who rescues us from Satan's power, from sin, from never-ending death. Our King does not deliver from bodily death; for earth is the place for suffering and dying, and He Himself had to suffer here and die. Those who recognize this character of the King and His kingdom bear the cross with resignation. For then they know that our Lord Jesus, the everlasting King, also had to bear the cross, and thus, remembering that the servant cannot fare better than his master, are made willing and ready to suffer. And, besides, they take comfort in the knowledge that, although they must suffer here, there in eternity joy and glory shall be theirs. It is this that makes Christians bold, even in the midst of temptation and death; while they who do not know these things cannot do otherwise in days of adversity than mourn, lament, murmur, show impatience, and, in the end, even despair. For the latter think that if God wished them well, He would not permit so much misery to come upon them, or else would soon help and rescue them. Such thoughts unmistakably prove that Christ is held to be a king of this world. Temporal kings must, according to the duties of their office, protect the bodies, lives and possessions of their subjects and defend them against danger. But Christ, the King of glory, permits body and property, life and all to be in danger.

Do thou learn and firmly believe that these things are so for the reason, simply, that His "Kingdom is not of this world." Thy Christian faith is not to be used by thee on earth as the means for obtaining all things in abundance, or for supplying all thy desires. For behold thy King! How does it fare with Him, the Lord Jesus? With what does He make a display? Did He live a life of ease? Do men regard Him as glorious? We see nothing there except the suffering, mocked, reviled and ignominiously slaughtered One.

True, He does sway a scepter, but only over a very small number, even the testimony of truth, that is, the holy Gospel. By means of this, as said already, He sends the Holy Spirit into the souls of men, forgives their sins, and gives them the hope of everlasting life. But all these things take place only in faith and in the Word; we cannot see them; we cannot touch them; they are realized not by reason, but by hope. However, when earth's kingdom ends and we dwell no longer here, then shall His kingdom and His glory be revealed to us, yea, we shall live with Him and with Him rule all things in heaven and on earth.

It was in this way that the Lord was recognized on the cross by one of the malefactors, saying, "Lord, remember me when Thou comest into

Thy kingdom." He saw Christ suspended on the tree in the same misery, in which he found himself. The malefactor on the left was offended at Christ's helplessness and helped the Jews to rail on Him: Ah! a very fine king, indeed! He concluded that since the dear Lord was so wretched and poor on earth, it would, of course, be useless to expect help from Him. But he on the right knew Him well; he knew Him not as a worldly, but as a spiritual and an eternal King. For this reason he prays that He would remember him in His kingdom when His body should be lifeless there upon the cross. In this way must we also believe in Him, and then shall we find immutable comfort in Christ Jesus.

Now, all Christians need that consolation which always, in all kinds of distress and disappointment, comes to them when they hold to Christ's confession before Pilate. It makes them say to themselves: Why shouldest thou weep? Why complain of this or that misfortune? Think what kind of a King thou hast; what says He before Pilate? "My kingdom is not of this world." Wouldst thou have thy kingdom here? No, no; for here it would not last; this is altogether the land of suffering! But in the world to come glory and a joyful life shall surely be found. If they could be found here, they would afford only a short and transient joy, for in this world there is nothing firm nor eternal. But Jesus Christ, my King, is a King in the other world, that is, an everlasting King; postpone thy glorying and thy pleasures, therefore, till thou goest thither, and be content with the treatment thou receivest here. Thy King has not given thee orders to remain here; He will have nothing to do with the world outside of the testimony of truth.—All Christians, I say, need this consolation, but especially they who hold the ministerial office and ply the Word.

For this reason St. Paul urges Timothy with these words, referring to Christ's confession before Pilate, to hold fast to the pure doctrine and not to let it be falsified. The world and the devil cannot bear the Word, and oppose it with all manner of confusion. Every pastor should and must, therefore, cling to the testimony mentioned, and recognize Christ as that King, in whom he finds comfort, and whom he hopes to enjoy,—but not on earth. He says, "But now is my kingdom not from hence." And again, "I am a king … for this cause came I into the world, that I should bear witness unto the truth." Whosoever, therefore, desires to have this King

Jesus, let him lay hold on the truth, which is His Word, and know that he shall not on account of His kingdom have greater abundance on earth; yea, let him know that he shall have to bear many a misfortune on account of the Word, even as did Christ, the King, Himself. But when life on earth is over, then shall come the full enjoyment of the Lord Jesus' kingdom.

The Pope and bishops never knew this consolation. They do not recognize as king one who does no more than bear witness unto the truth, and cry with Pilate: "What is truth?" Had we nothing else we would, no doubt, have to go a begging. Therefore will we have another king,—one who can give us plenty of money, possessions, honor, power and everything; as for this King and His truth, they may in the meanwhile fare as they can. But St. Paul cautions against such folly. And every pious pastor should earnestly heed this admonition, and depend upon it that we shall not be glorified on earth, and that all our glory here shall be to bear witness unto the truth. Earth's reward for this service shall be in our case what it was in the Lord Jesus' case, the gallows and the executioner. Learn to suffer and to hear such things, and let it be your faith and hope, that, although you must suffer here, still this suffering shall, in the other world, be rewarded and made good by the Lord Jesus, the eternal King! But this must suffice for a brief consideration of the testimony before Pilate.

We must now examine the third point also. It is this: Pilate and the Jews greatly undervalue the blood of our dear Lord Jesus, which, finally, falls on them as a crushing and eternal burden.

Matthew mentions in particular that Pilate washed his hands before the multitude, and said: "I am innocent of the blood of this just person." He thought he had done his whole duty in making several attempts to liberate Christ, and that he could not help it that the Jews resisted him in his efforts. Still he delivered the Lord to be crucified. Just as though his saying "I am innocent" would make him innocent! Had he desired a warning, his wife might have told him how innocent he would be; for she, as related above in the text, had spent a whole night suffering many things in a dream, from which she could judge the severity of the judgment which Pilate would bring upon himself and all belonging to him by consenting to the death of "that just man." But so it always is with the blood of the Lord Jesus and with that of His Christians. Herod the elder slew all Bethlehem's innocent infants. His son slew the holy John the Baptist. Both dared to think themselves benefited by their murder. Neither did Pilate here regard it as much out of the way that he sentenced Christ to die. He thought that his opinion would also be God's opinion, and that God would, therefore, hold him innocent. But without doubt God's wrath did not tarry long till it utterly destroyed the house, the tribe, the name of Pilate, and then thrust his body and soul into hell and into the eternal fire. There he discovered how innocent he was of this blood!

But the Jews went about this murder with still greater recklessness. When Pilate said, "See ye to it," they shamelessly burst out with the cry, "His blood be on us, and on our children," that is, in case He should be wronged, we are willing that we and our children shall suffer for it. It was easily said, and seemed to have been spoken with impunity. But before forty years had passed they saw their imprecation about to be answered. And then this "blood" began to flow down upon them in such streams that Jerusalem and the whole Jewish kingdom soon were desolate, the people lamentably slain, and all things overthrown. But even this sufficed not; from that time till this, and it is now nearly fifteen hundred years, they have wandered about in misery, nowhere finding a continuing city.

This temporal punishment, so that they have no cities nor government of their own, is truly severe, but it shall come to an end. But this is truly terrible that their hearts are so horribly imbittered against Christ, the Son of God. Instead of seeking and expecting forgiveness of sin and eternal life and salvation, as they should, of Christ, their King and God, they abuse and revile Him, thus taking delight in falsehood and error, and diligently seek means of darkening the Scriptures before their own eyes and preventing their understanding it. Therefore, when they fancy that they are calling upon and serving God, they really serve the very devil. Neither does God hear them. And since they desire no freedom from sin through the Son of God, there can be nothing surer to them than that they must die in their sins and be forever ruined. In the 8. chapter of John, Christ tells them this very thing: "If ye believe not that I am He, ye shall die in your sins."

They did not, at that time, perceive this calamity, and even thought that the sooner Christ could be slain the better it would be for them. Without any further thought, therefore, they said: If He is wronged, may we and our children be punished! But even as the thirty pieces of silver afforded Judas a joy of only short duration, so also a change soon came upon the Jews. From day to day failure advanced upon all their affairs, until, in the end, they went to utter ruin. This is, therefore, a fit subject for the serious meditation especially of great kings and princes; these should remember what an easy, trifling thing it seemed for Pilate and the Jews to shed innocent blood, and how this finally forced them into the abyss of hell.

When our bishops and their idol, the Pope, have succeeded in seizing a pious, faithful minister and pastor, they hurry him off to the stake or to the gallows, and dream they have done well; they do this, therefore, like Pilate and the Jews, with wantonness. But their success is not made certain yet; alas, such an end as theirs shall be! For it is impossible that God should look long upon such deeds in silence; innocent blood cries so mightily into His ears that He must rise and inflict punishment.

Pilate was thrust so low that now, no doubt, not a single person of his name or tribe remains. The Jews to this day are laboring under the blood of Jesus Christ, and it will finally press them down to hell. The great and powerful emperors and the mighty princes in the Romish and all other kingdoms, and everyone else that has ever persecuted Christians,—they all have been lamentably overthrown and slain.

And surely the same fate awaits the enemies of Christ of our day, who act as tyrants and persecute and murder Christians for the Gospel's sake. Let no one fear that punishment shall fail to come! They who meddle with the innocent blood of Christians, though they may be as mighty as the Emperor Augustus, must still go down, together with all their descendants. They may, indeed, be thinking now that we are heretics and that they do right by slaying us. So thought Pilate, and especially the Jews, but it availed them nothing. Let everyone, therefore, take good care of himself and let alone the blood of Christians! At first it seems a little sin,—a trifle merely; but in the end, everything that is stained with Christians' blood shall be utterly destroyed, as all history testifies.

May Almighty God resist all tyrants, mercifully grant peace unto His Church, graciously keep us by His Word and save us forever. Amen.

9

Christ Led away to be Crucified.—Simon Bears the Cross after Him.—The Women who Follow Bewail and Lament Him

As the soldiers led him away, they seized Simon from Cyrene, who was on his way in from the country, and put the cross on him and made him carry it behind Jesus. A large number of people followed him, including women who mourned and wailed for him. Jesus turned and said to them, "Daughters of Jerusalem, do not weep for me; weep for yourselves and for your children. For the time will come when you will say, 'Blessed are the childless women, the wombs that never bore and the breasts that never nursed!' Then "'they will say to the mountains, "Fall on us!" and to the hills, "Cover us!"' For if people do these things when the tree is green, what will happen when it is dry?"

—LUKE 23:26–31

Simon's bearing the cross and the women's weeping occurred while Christ was being led from Pilate to the place of execution. Matthew, Mark and Luke alike make mention of Simon, a Cyrenian, to show, no doubt, that what is said of him was no accident, as it might seem, but so ordained by God for a special purpose, viz.: that at the very time when Christ should be led away to suffer, all Christians might have an example set, from which to learn how they should fare on earth,—that they must bear the cross after the Lord Jesus, like Simon here. This good and pious man, not knowing in what the Jews at Jerusalem were engaged, went into the city according to his need and opportunity, to attend to his business. And now, as the Lord and the two murderers were led toward him, and the Lord, on account of weakness, could carry no further the cross which had been placed on Him, and which, since a strong, full-grown man was to be nailed to it, must have been pretty heavy, the soldiers ran up to good, pious Simon and compelled him to take up the cross or tree, to which Christ was to be nailed, and to bear it after the Lord.

This looks as if it had happened incidentally. But it is, as already said, a picture of all Christians, which God wished to show to His Church just when His dear Son, Jesus Christ, was Himself suffering, so as to check that common offence which is so apt to lead us all astray. For as soon as God comes to us with the cross, attacking our body or property, giving us ill-bred children or sending some other misfortune or calamity, our courage fails us. We then conclude that God does not wish us well, and that if He loved us He would deal more gently with us. We take the fact that He permits us to be troubled, afflicted and tormented as an indication that He is angry with us and refuses to be gracious.

Now, the picture in our text is to operate against offences of this kind. In the first place, we see the Son of God bearing His cross Himself and finding it so heavy that it nearly throws Him down and that He can scarcely walk. Mark this well! For if such things happen to the green and fruitful tree, about which we shall soon be told, it is easy to infer that better things shall not and cannot happen the dry and unfruitful tree. In the second place, we see pious Simon doing the work that others should have done; had he not come near where Christ was compelled to carry His cross, he would never have needed to bear a cross. But here he suffers for the Lord Jesus; because Christ carries the cross, he also must suffer and help to carry it. Remember, it shall never be different with Christians here; they must all submit with Simon and bear the cross after Christ.

Although God may bear with the wicked for a while and permit them to receive everything that their hearts wish and covet, still their punishment shall not be delayed always. They too must suffer here on earth, receiving now here a kick then there a thrust, and never afterward enjoying uninterrupted success, as the 32. Psalm tells us: "Many sorrows shall be to the wicked; but he that trusteth in the Lord, mercy shall compass him about," and as is glaringly shown by examples.

Severe and violent were the sufferings of ungodly Pharaoh and his Egyptians. And how much misfortune, oppression and grief did not the Jews have to bear in the desert and afterward in the land of Canaan, until, finally, the Assyrian wasted the ten tribes, and, some time after, even Judah's tribe was flung into the whirlpool of woes and the entire land conquered by the Babylonians! But it is not necessary to cite many instances. Each one need merely think of what he himself has seen and experienced in his own case and in that of others. It is, therefore, impossible that punishment, distress, wretchedness and tribulation should finally fail to follow where God is not feared and where His Word and will are resisted.

But from the case of Simon here we must learn to make a difference between the holy cross and the well-deserved punishment and misery of the wicked. No wonder if the knave fares badly; for he rushes to his doom with open eyes. If the thief would stop his stealing he would, no doubt, remain secure against the gallows and the hangman. As for men and women, if they would refrain from debauchery, they might enjoy wealth, honor and health. But since they do not desist, but continue in sin, God punishes them with poverty, disgrace, disease, or other misfortunes. These wicked ones wish nothing else and nothing better; for by their sin and impenitent lives they themselves furnish the cause for their misery and distress; they urge God, who would delight in being merciful and in giving them all good things, yea, they compel Him to make His anger burn at once, to heap destruction on them and to stem the tide of sin. Peter therefore says, 1 Pet. 4:15: "But let none of you suffer as a murderer, or as a thief, or as an evil-doer, or as a busybody in other men's matters." He thus makes this distinction, that not all suffering is to be called a "cross;" for that which the wicked suffer is not their cross, but their punishment and merited reward; while that which Christians suffer, like Simon here, is called and is in reality a "cross," because it is not merited, but the fault of others. If Simon had not just happened to meet the Lord Jesus, he would have been let alone; but he has to suffer for it that he came where Christ was being led to the crucifixion.

In this way all Christians should suffer and bear the cross; even as Peter says: Not "suffer as a murderer, or as a thief, … yet … as a Christian," that is, for the sake of the Lord Jesus and His Word and confession. All Christians acknowledge themselves to be poor sinners, and know that through sin they have deserved all the calamities God sends upon them on earth, and many more. They are, indeed, the only ones who acknowledge their short-comings, weakness and transgressions; for sin's peculiar punishment is eternal death, and not this or that particular temporal misfortune. Nevertheless, their suffering is not the punishment for sin, but the real and holy "cross." His being a sinner and his stumbling and falling occasionally, is not the reason why the Christian is hated by the evil adversary and the world. No, both the devil and the world could well tolerate that, and would be satisfied with the Christian as far as that is concerned. But the Christian holds to the Word and has faith; he put his hope in Christ, the Son of God, and is comforted in His death and resurrection; he fears God and tries to live according to His will; he labors hard, by means of his confession, to persuade others to believe and to come to the knowledge of Christ. This it is that neither the devil nor his tender bride, the world, can endure; this it is that makes Satan rage so terribly against all Christians; this it is that makes him always pursue them, afflicting their bodies with disease and sometimes their property with loss by storms, or hail, or fire, as it was the case with Job. (Job 1.) And sometimes he troubles them with great secret torments of conscience, such as melancholy, sadness, fear, trembling, doubts, dread of death, and like fiery darts of the devil, about which the Psalms lament so much. Of this kind was the temptation of Paul which he mentions 2 Cor. 12: "There was given to me a thorn in the flesh, the messenger of Satan to buffet me," &c. And what the world does in this direction is easily seen, especially in times like the present, when poor Christians receive such wretched and horrible treatment.

This is bearing the Lord Jesus' cross as Simon did. Simon was certainly also a poor sinner, but what is that to these soldiers? It is not for this that they make him suffer, but they make him suffer because Christ, who cannot get along with His cross, is present and needs someone to help Him bear the cross.

Therefore, although thou art a poor sinner, and confessest how thou hast in various ways sinned against God; still, because thou believest in Christ, thy sins are not the chief cause of all thy crosses and afflictions, and thy sins are not that for which the devil and the world punish thee. Nay, it would be their joy and rejoicing if thou wouldst be altogether on their side, and not on that of God and His Word. It is chiefly on account of the Lord Jesus, His Word and thy faith that thou must suffer.

This, that Simon bears the Lord Jesus' cross, is the first thing to be learned here. It is profitable especially for consolation, giving us certainty that we shall realize our hope of help and salvation, and provoking us to prayer. For he who, when he lies under the cross and in misery, thinks only of his being a sinner and deserving such punishment, is, by such thoughts, made too cold and too lazy to pray. For it is the nature of sin always to terrify the heart, to make it fearful and timid, and to deprive it of the consolation and the hope that God will bestow aught that is good. But if we consider the real, chief reason why the devil and the world are such bitter enemies of ours and heap all manner of mischief on us, we shall have to confess that it is not on account of our sins that they are so furious. They would like, and this is their constant aim, to plunge us into all sin and shame, to succeed in which would be their pleasure and satisfaction. They are opposed to us, they seek where they can to do us harm and hate us, especially because we heed the Word of God, confess the Lord Jesus, place our confidence in the goodness and grace of God and desire to live according to His will, in His fear and love, and in faith and obedience. This is the fountain and foundation of their hatred and envy. Mark well, thou must therefore not deny that thou art a poor sinner, and that thou hast by thy sins deserved every calamity. For God punishes also His own for their sins, as Peter says, "Judgment must begin at the house of God." But Satan and the world, so say to thyself, are not angry with me on this account; they would be satisfied with me if I, like a hog in the mire, remained impenitent in my sins. But why, then, do they hate me? Simply because I believe and confess that the Man who here bears the cross is my God and Savior.

Now, if this is true, what shall we do next? Shall we despair? No, as you prize your soul, no! Firm hope must be ours. And though we are miserable sinners, it is still most sure that the Lord Jesus will not let us perish as long as we suffer for His sake. He can help us mercifully, and He will do so. And as we suffer and die with Him, so shall we also be exalted with Him into glory and live with Him forever. But let us boldly open our mouth and cry, saying: O Lord, we are, indeed, poor sinners, and by our disobedience have deserved infinitely severer chastisement than we are now bearing; but look, O Lord, at the wicked enemy's intentions. The enemy hates Thee and Thy name, and hates us too because we hold fast to Thee and Thy name, find comfort in Thy Word, and hope for mercy through Thy death and merits. Therefore, dear Lord Jesus Christ, be Thou avenged on them, and help us for Thy name's sake.—Such thoughts make the heart cheerful and give it confidence and boldness to pour itself out in prayer. For this reason the holy Prophets also prayed in this way, constantly pleading the name of God, as David does in the 44. Psalm: "Yea, for Thy sake are we killed all day long; we are counted as sheep for the slaughter." Let the preceding, about Simon's being compelled by the soldiers to suffer for the sake of the Lord Jesus by bearing His cross, be said, then, for the special purpose of teaching the distinction between the Christian's cross and the wicked man's punishment for sin.

The second thing to be learned here is that Simon not only bears the cross, but also bears it because he is compelled to do so. For if he would have had his own will in the matter, he would have gone his way and cared very little what was becoming of Christ and His cross. But the soldiers seize him against his will, and compel him to carry the cross.

This subject teaches us also very nicely what really is and what is not a cross. Monks and nuns who are in earnest, lead an austere life and oppress themselves with the most difficult labor. But this is not the cross of Christ which Simon bears. Why? Because they have placed it on themselves from their own free choice and without the command of God. And just so the Anabaptists do. But the proverb, "what is done from choice is done with ease," might be applied to such suffering; since it is self-imposed, and might be avoided, it cannot hurt very badly. But when one is compelled to bear the cross and does it reluctantly, then it becomes heavy and oppressive. It is this idea that Christ expresses when He says, John 21, to Peter: "When thou wast young, thou girdedst thyself, and walkedst whither thou wouldest; but when thou shalt be old, thou shalt stretch forth thy hands, and another shall gird thee, and carry thee whither thou wouldest not." Let Christians be ever so perfect, flesh and blood cannot help but shudder at, fear and shun the cross.

For this reason this man is called Simon or Simeon, which, in his language, means one who takes advice and obeys. For that is true obedience which, though it prefers to be exempt from this or that suffering, still yields to it willingly, following and letting itself be led, simply because it sees that God desires it so. All true Christians can be called by this name Simon. For although their flesh and blood would like to rest and be excused from pain, they still obey, heed the Word, are submissive to to the will of God, and help the Lord Jesus bear His cross.

The third thing to be learned here is to distinguish between Simon and the Lord Jesus. Simon bears the cross after the Lord Jesus as far as the place of execution and then goes away; while Christ allows Himself to be nailed to the cross and dies on it. This is the true difference between the suffering of Christ and our suffering. Our suffering does not earn the forgiveness of sins. This is accomplished alone by the sufferings of our Lord Jesus. He alone is the true Sacrifice and Lamb of God which pays and atones for the sins of all the world and, for this reason, hangs upon the cross. But Simon merely carries the cross; that is, our bearing the cross does nothing more with the old Adam than molest him, and nothing more with sin than oppose it. But it is the work and merit of our Lord Jesus alone that forgives our sins.

Thus, beloved, you perceive that this Simon is a pattern for all Christians, for they must bear the cross of the Lord Jesus; and that it is not, however, on account of this bearing that their sins are forgiven. The bearing of the cross serves to restrain the old Adam, lest he become too wild. But when the cross is to be the means of the forgiveness of sins, it will not do for Simon to bear it, but then Christ must hang and die on it. This is the reason why Simon is set free. By Christ's death we are set free from death and receive eternal life, as this is clearly pointed out in that part of our text which we are about to treat.

St. Luke tells us that as the Lord was led out of Jerusalem, some women followed, bewailing and lamenting Him. The Lord turned to them and told them not to weep for Him, but for themselves and for their children, because the time was coming when the woman without child would be called blessed, and when, as Hosea says, men would desire the mountains to fall upon and cover them. But the reason of such calamity and woe was, that since Christ, the green tree, was so badly treated, they, the dry and barren tree, would be treated still worse.

Although these things referred especially to the Jews of that day, they still show us how to make proper use of our Lord Jesus' sufferings; first, by revealing sin as a terrible burden,—the Son of God Himself being compelled to die on account of our sin; and then, by consoling us against sin by means of Christ's sufferings,—the Son of God having rendered satisfaction and atoned for sin upon the cross.

Notice, first, the difference which the Lord makes between Himself and the Jews, for on this difference a great deal depends. Himself He compares to a young tree, so beautiful and fruitful that it should be bought for a garden, and by no means cut down and cast into the fire. Nevertheless, the latter is done. God lets Him be cut down, that is, He lets Him now be led out to the cross, where He is to be slain as the greatest malefactor, notwithstanding that He is such a fine, sappy, beautiful and fruitful tree. He is without all sin and walks before God in perfect obedience, and all things He says and does are purely noble and precious fruits, every one of which is a joy to God and a blessing to us. In short, we find nothing about the Lord Jesus that is not grace, life and salvation. The Jews on the other hand, He compares to an old, barren, dry and rotten tree, which is altogether out of place in the garden, and only fit to be felled and burned. For they did not heed God's Word. John's preaching brought no fruit; they said John had a devil. Christ, the Son of God, Himself and His Apostles preached. Neither did they pay any attention to Him, but called Him a wine-bibber, said He had a devil, and hated and envied Him so bitterly that they had no peace until they had brought Him from life to death. Nevertheless, since they had Moses, the law, and the external worship of God in the temple at Jerusalem, they dared to think that they were God's people, that they were living saints, indeed, and that they rested in God's bosom. Now, it is easy to imagine, if the Son of God, who is a fine, fruitful tree, is visited by so severe a judgment of God, how infinitely severe shall be the fate of the terribly great sinners, the dry trees. It was the Lord's desire that the Jews should understand this now and not continue in their sin; that, by seeing Him, who, though innocent, was crucified and killed, they might learn to fear the wrath of God and to flee from it by true repentance. Little, however, did this warning avail. The dry tree could yield no fruit, and so was cast into the fire. History shows this, where it tells us that about forty years after Christ's death a most terrible judgment came upon the Jews for their sin, the Romans desolating their whole land. For themselves, therefore, even as the Lord here counsels and exhorts them to do, and not for Christ, should they have wept, acknowledging their sins and repenting.

We too, however, should take this advice to heart. For we all must confess that we have many and great sins and, therefore, are dry and unfruitful trees,—trees which do not and can not yield anything good. What, then, shall we do? Nothing except weep and cry to God for pardon, and earnestly resist and curb our evil, sinful nature and inordinate desires. For we are admonished here, that since the fruitful tree receives such shameful treatment, God permitting His dear Son to suffer so severely, we should not feel secure, nor laugh, nor skip carelessly along, like the world, which neither hears nor knows this warning of the Lord. But we should weep, we should discern our sins, we should heartily lament that we have been so corrupted by sin and that we have become unfruitful trees; we should fear the wrath of God on this account and pray for mercy and forgiveness.

The first thing for us specially to learn from the sufferings of Christ is to fear God and His anger on account of our sins, and not to give the reins to sin. This we must do for ourselves, for we are a dry, unfruitful tree, which is fit only for the fire.

But the Lord teaches us still another thing here. We should weep for ourselves and for our children; but for Him we should not weep, but laugh, rejoice and be of good cheer. For why does He suffer? He is a genuine, good and fruitful tree, and has not deserved such a cruel fate, but bears it for our sin's sake. And as He now proceeds to the cross it is His only aim to perform the work of His priestly office, and not only to pray for sinners, but also to sacrifice His body and His life upon the altar of the cross for them, so that this offering may reconcile God, liberate poor sinners from His wrath, and make them heirs of everlasting life. The Lord, therefore, does not want us to think of His sufferings as of something for which we should weep. He wants us to rejoice, to glorify God, to thank Him for His mercy, to praise, to extol and to confess Him, because His going to the cross has brought to us the grace of God, freed us from sin and death, and made us God's dear children.

But the first of these lessons goes down as hard with us as the second, and the second as hard as the first. We prefer the ways of the world to the warning and advice of the Lord Jesus. We should weep for ourselves, because sin has polluted us so, and because so terrible a judgment awaits us. But where is the man to be found who weeps? The deeper men sink into the slime of sin, the more secure and joyful they grow. Man deems his joy, glory and life perfect, as we have said several times before, when he has numerous occasions for sinning. No sum of money can satiate the miser's maw. The more advantage the greedy man can take and the freer access to gain he has, the happier he becomes, and he verily imagines that he has done his work well. Just so it is with other sins, such as anger, lewdness, envy, pride. Who cares for them? Who weeps for them? They are loved by every one and every one yields to them.

How the Jews succeeded with such work we clearly see. It behooves us, therefore, to repent and, as the Lord now so faithfully exhorts when He is about to die, to be concerned and grieved for ourselves. And it is certain, once for all, that our sins shall be punished with eternal death unless we are freed from them.

Even as we are disobedient with reference to the first lesson, for no one weeps and none lament their sins; so do we disobey in regard to the second, for no one wishes heartily to rejoice over the dear Lord Jesus. Money, possessions, honor and the like, mean and little though they be, rejoice the heart; while that which is exclusively grace and life and salvation finds the heart almost chilled and dead, and void of all longing and desire and heartfelt eagerness to possess this treasure.

These lessons, when attention is paid merely to their words, are, indeed, easily and quickly learned; but when, on the other hand, they are to be mastered in their relation to our heart and sinful nature, the task is most difficult and even impossible. Our determination to invert these lessons is hereditary. Instead of weeping for our sins, we laugh about them. Instead of laughing and exulting with all our heart that Christ has died for us, we weep. Now, we either regard this rejoicing on account of Jesus as not superior to the more popular joys of the world; or else sin and the wrath of God have seized our souls and banished from them the desire and the ability to be comforted. Christ's "Weep not for me" hardly penetrates the heart. We weep and lament and despair as though Christ had not died, not paid for our sins, not averted God's anger, and not delivered us from death.

Before either lesson can be learned, therefore, prayer is necessary. We must pray, first, that God, by His Holy Spirit, would move our hearts, disgust us with and dissuade us from sin, and shield us from false security. We must pray, again, that He would kindle in our souls the flame of consolation against sin, and seal there the confidence in the sacrifice and satisfaction of Christ Jesus; so that we may truly worship God, like poor sinners fear Him, abide in repentance and trust in His goodness with all our heart; for He does not wish us harm, seeing that for the forgiveness of our sins He delivered His Only Begotten into death, even the death of the cross. May our dear Lord Jesus grant us this. Amen.

10

Christ Nailed to the Cross— His Deeds, Sufferings and Words on the Cross

They came to a place called Golgotha (which means "the place of the skull"). There they offered Jesus wine to drink, mixed with gall; but after tasting it, he refused to drink it. When they had crucified him, they divided up his clothes by casting lots. And sitting down, they kept watch over him there. Above his head they placed the written charge against him: THIS IS JESUS, THE KING OF THE JEWS. Two rebels were crucified with him, one on his right and one on his left. Those who passed by hurled insults at him, shaking their heads and saying, "You who are going to destroy the temple and build it in three days, save yourself! Come down from the cross, if you are the Son of God!" In the same way the chief priests, the teachers of the law and the elders mocked him. "He saved others," they said, "but he can't save himself! He's the king of Israel! Let him come down now from the cross, and we will believe in him. He trusts in God. Let God rescue him now if he wants him, for he said, 'I am the Son of God.'" In the same way the rebels who were crucified with him also heaped insults on him. From noon until three in the afternoon darkness came over all the land. About three in the afternoon Jesus cried out in a loud voice, "Eli, Eli, lema sabachthani?" (which means "My God, my God, why have you forsaken me?"). When some of those standing there heard this, they said, "He's calling Elijah." Immediately one of them ran and got a sponge. He filled it with wine vinegar, put it on a staff, and offered it to Jesus to drink. The rest said, "Now leave him alone. Let's see if Elijah comes to save him." And when Jesus had cried out again in a loud voice, he gave up his spirit. At that moment the curtain of the temple was torn in two from top to bottom. The earth shook, the rocks split and the tombs broke open. The bodies of many holy people who had died were raised to life. They came out of the tombs after Jesus' resurrection and went into the holy city and appeared to many people. When the centurion and those with him who were guarding Jesus saw the earthquake and all that had happened, they were terrified, and exclaimed, "Surely he was the Son of God!" Many women were there, watching from a distance. They had followed Jesus from Galilee to care for his needs. Among them were Mary Magdalene, Mary the mother of James and Joseph, and the mother of Zebedee's sons.

—**MATTHEW 27:33–56**

Each of the four Evangelists makes a record of the things that occurred on the cross. Still, sometimes one of them mentions a thing that the rest of them omit. Before treating, therefore, on the true doctrine taught in our text, we propose to recite the history of the cross in its details as furnished by all four Evangelists.

When the soldiers had brought the Lord Jesus to Golgotha, the place for executing public malefactors, "they gave Him," as Matthew relates, "vinegar to drink mingled with gall." This gall was not the gall of a live beast, but a compound of all sorts of bitter herbs. This drink, as some suppose, was given to dying criminals, to hasten their departure. But the Lord would not drink of it, for He had willingly yielded to this death. The word gall is used in this sense in Deut. 29, Ps. 69, Jer. 8, and in other places. Immediately after this, the soldiers nailed Him to the cross and two malefactors with Him, one on His right and one on His left. The Lord Jesus, however, as the true priest who must now attend to His priestly office, prayed for those who crucified Him and for all poor sinners, saying: "Father, forgive them; for they know not what they do." We shall have occasion to see the fruit of this prayer when we come to speak of the malefactor on the right of Christ; for to him it was that Gospel and sermon, from which he learned to know Christ as the Son of God, that He hanged upon the cross as the atonement for the sins of the whole world, and that after His bodily death He would live and reign with God, His Father, in eternity.

The Evangelists announce that Pilate placed the superscription, "Jesus of Nazareth, the King of the Jews," written in three languages, over the head of the Lord Jesus. It was customary to do this, so that everyone might know why people were executed, and take warning. The superscription over the head of the Lord Jesus was to serve the special purpose of admonishing the Jews, even while He was hanging miserably on the cross, not to be offended in Him, but to take Him for their King. But it was in vain! The title made them so indignant that they accosted Pilate thus: "Write not, The King of the Jews; but that He said, I am the King of the Jews." But Pilate was much displeased with them and would not alter the superscription, which remains an eternal testimony against the Jews, that they could not rest until they had crucified their King.

Hereupon the soldiers, four in number, took the Lord Jesus' garments, separating them into four parts. His coat, however, which was without seam, being woven, they did not rend, but cast lots for it. And John says that this had been prophesied in the Scriptures. He would have us understand by this that the taking of the Lord's garments was no accident, but done by God's special counsel, that it might serve the Church as an emblem; for it shows, first, that the world is not satisfied even when it has put Christians to death, but takes what little property Christians may have and plunders them. This we can see in our old histories, where Julian and other bloodhounds and tyrants drove poor Christians away from their possessions and took from them what they had. We see it not there only, but we have living instances of tyrants and bishops who are well enough pleased when their subjects, contrary to their command, eat meat, hear Lutheran (as they call them) sermons, receive both bread and wine in the Sacrament, and the like; for then they have plausible reasons to oppress their subjects, to sell or trespass upon their property, or to tax them as they please. But we can also see how much richer such money makes them. Money thus unrighteously extorted devours all they have, so that afterward they are neither blest nor prosperous.

The soldiers' casting lots upon the vesture of the Lord can, no doubt, be applied to sects and heretics. The Holy Scriptures is the coat which our Lord Jesus puts on, and in which He can be seen and found. This coat is woven throughout, and all its threads are so interlocked that it cannot be cut nor divided. But the soldiers who crucify Christ, that is, heretics and sects, interest themselves in this coat. Their chief fault is that they want the whole coat, that is, that they try to convince everyone that all Scripture harmonizes with them and their opinions. She Sacramentarians of our day serve as an illustration. They regard the words, "This is my body," "This is my blood," as insignificant, saying that they are only a single passage, while the Bible, as they boast, is full of passages which prove Christ to be no longer on earth, but in heaven.

The manner of all sects is to adopt a special opinion without consulting the Word; this opinion then hangs continually before their eyes, like blue glasses, and everything they see is blue, that is, according to their own opinion. But they are knaves, as St. Paul calls them, Eph. 4, where he admonishes us to be no more "carried about with every wind of doctrine, by the sleight of men, and cunning craftiness, whereby they lie in wait to deceive." The Greek word here translated "sleight" is *kybia*, which means, in English, playing at dice, or trickery. Now, as the knave masters the die so that it must fall to suit him, so sects and fanatics master the Word. Everyone wants the whole of it, and makes use of the die. But let us proceed with the history.

As the Lord was hanging on the cross He saw His mother and His mother's sister and John with them, and "He saith unto His mother, Woman, behold thy Son! Then saith He to the disciple, Behold thy mother!"

After this, men of every station began the most heartless scoffing. The chief priests, scribes and elders, as Matthew writes, said, "He saved others; let Him save Himself, if He be Christ, the chosen of God." With such pointed, poisonous words they wished not only to insult the Lord, but also to alienate from Him the people, so that they would not respect Him, so that they would slight and despise all the miracles they had seen and all the sermons they had heard, and so that they would regard Him as a blasphemer. The soldiers, who as Gentiles cared not about God, mocked Him in a different way, giving Him vinegar to drink, "and saying, If Thou be the King of the Jews, save Thyself."

Finally, even one of the malefactors "railed on Him, saying, If Thou be Christ, save Thyself and us." But the other rebuked him for this, saying: And dost even thou not fear God? There thou hangest and in less than an hour or two all will be over with thee. Thou hast all thy life been a scoundrel, like myself, and hast well deserved this punishment. Is it not high time to think of thy salvation and to leave such foolish words unspoken? After giving this reproof he turned to the Lord and said, "Remember me when Thou comest into Thy kingdom." And Jesus answered, "Verily, I say unto thee, To-day shalt thou be with me in paradise."

In the meantime came deep darkness, most unnatural and terrible. The agony of death pressed from the Lord the cry: "My God, my God, why hast Thou forsaken me?" The Jews well enough understood the meaning of this cry; still their bitterness and their fierceness urged them to pervert Christ's word and say: "This man calleth for Elias.... Let be, let us see whether Elias will come to save Him!"

"Jesus knowing that all things were now accomplished, that the Scripture might be fulfilled, saith, I thirst." Then the soldiers took a sponge filled "with vinegar, and put it upon hyssop, and put it to His mouth. When Jesus therefore had received the vinegar, He said, It is finished." By these words He meant to say: The world and the devil have now done all that lies in their power, and therefore I have now done all that the redemption of mankind demands, and all that the Prophets have foretold in Holy Writ; the work is done! Then He "cried with a loud voice, ... Father, into Thy hands I commend my spirit; and having said thus, He gave up the ghost."

Immediately after, "the vail of the temple was rent in twain from the top to the bottom," as a testimony that the proper offering had been made to God at last, and that now the law and its sacrifices, which were merely a type of the sacrifice just made, were forever abrogated. The temple was so constructed that the people stood to hear the Word of God and to sing and pray in the apartment nearest the entrance. This was separated from another apartment, which was similar to the chancels in some of our churches, into which were admitted only the priests, who there offered sacrifices and did the other things belonging to the service of God, and which, because none except the holy priests dared enter there, was called the holy place. Beyond this was still another apartment, called the holy of holies, in which stood the mercy seat. This was separated from the holy place by means of a vail, beyond which no one was allowed to go except the high priest, and he only once every year, when he offered for his sins and for the sins of all the people. It is this vail that the Evangelists tell us was rent. They mention this to testify to us that God's services, as they were conducted in the holy of holies, are ended and abolished, and this because the highest priest, God's Son, has offered now unto God, His Father, for the sins of the whole world, not the blood of goats and calves, but His own body and blood.

This rending of the vail took place while the earth quaked so violently that the rocks rent and that the graves of numerous saints were opened. Out of these graves, after the resurrection of Christ, arose many bodies of the saints, who appeared unto many in Jerusalem, who preached concerning the Lord Jesus and who testified that He was Christ, the true Messiah. These ascended to heaven with the Lord Jesus to live there forever, like Enoch and Elias, whom God took into heaven alive, the former before the flood and the latter three thousand years after the creation of the world. God desired to preserve to His Church in every age a sure testimony of the resurrection from the dead. The number was greater, however, in the case before us than it had ever been in any other case.

Now when the centurion, who had to remain at the cross, and others, saw the earthquake and the other unusual "things that were done, they feared greatly, saying, Truly this was the Son of God." "And all the people that came together to that sight, beholding the things which were done, smote their breasts, and returned."

All this, according to the Evangelists, took place at the cross before Christ expired. But we cannot consider the whole of it in one sermon. For the present, therefore, we shall confine ourselves to two points. First, why the Evangelists quote more Scripture when they give the history of the passion than on any other subject. Secondly, why God destined His Son to die upon the cross.

The Evangelists cite so many Scripture passages for every part of the history of Christ's sufferings, in order to combat the offence occasioned at sight of these sufferings, which must have sorely tried the disciples in particular. Not only the unbelieving Jews, but even the disciples of Jesus were offended at Christ's dying such a miserable and ignominious death. Both the Jews and the disciples thought that if this were Christ He would surely build up again the poor, oppressed and ruined kingdom. Why, even after Christ's resurrection the disciples continued to think in this way, for they lamented that the Lord was about to ascend to heaven and depart from the earth, and at the mount of Olives they asked Him, "Lord, wilt Thou at this time restore again the kingdom to Israel?"

When the Lord had now fallen into the hands of His enemies and had suffered Himself to be slain on the cross, all the hopes which the disciples had entertained for His glory vanished. The two disciples who went to Emmaus freely confessed this, saying: "We trusted that it had been He which should have redeemed Israel," as if they would say: It is all over now; we hoped for things different from those which we have realized. The Jews were offended still more seriously; for, because the Lord was dying so shamefully and would not save Himself, they regarded Him, in spite of His miracles and sermons, as an impostor, and tauntingly demanded that He should come down from the cross if He were the Son of God, so that they might believe in Him. The Jews hated Jesus, the disciples loved Him; the Jews rejoiced in His misfortune, the disciples were saddened and discouraged by it. Notwithstanding that they were thus differently disposed toward Christ, they all, both disciples and Jews, thought that it was all over with Him now and that He was not the true Messiah.

But how must we account for this opinion and for such offence? Simply thus: they left the Scriptures out of sight and had not diligently studied the Prophets. For it is written in the Prophets, Isa. 53, that the Messiah must suffer and die. The Scriptures, Isa. 53, declare that He should be "numbered with the transgressors." In the 41. Ps. and in the 11. chap. of Zech. we are told that His "own familiar friend" should betray Him and sell Him for "thirty pieces of silver." The 22. Ps. plainly tells us that the soldiers should part His garments among them, and cast lots upon His vesture, while the 69. declares that when He shall thirst in His agony upon the cross they shall give Him vinegar to drink. It had been prophesied that there should not a bone of Him be broken and that a spear should pierce His side, Ex. 12, Zech. 12, &c. Now, if the disciples and the Jews had carefully studied the writings of the Prophets, instead of finding cause for offence in Christ's sufferings and scandalous death, they would have found comfort therein. If they had studied the Scriptures, the fact that it came to pass just as the Holy Spirit, who cannot lie nor err, through the Prophets and in the Psalms, had predicted concerning Christ, would have led them to the firm conclusion that this was the Messiah indeed. But they gave no heed to the Scriptures, and therefore could not resist the offence which, like a flood, swept them away, so that they entirely lost Christ.

The Apostles personally experienced the disadvantage of departing from the Scriptures and not following them, and therefore continually quote the Scriptures as they write the history of the passion. By so doing they would say: It seems ridiculous that the crucified Jesus, who hangs there so miserably upon the cross, and who was treated so unmercifully and with such excessive wantonness by the soldiers, should be the Son of God and the true Messiah. But let us not be offended in Him! If we notice what the Holy Spirit had predicted long before through the Prophets concerning the Messiah, we shall find that this Jesus is the true Messiah, and that He bore what had been appointed for the Messiah to bear. It is most certainly true that if we do not hold to the Word we shall not be able to defend ourselves against the least offence. We are lost unless we take refuge in the Word.

Everyone should, for this reason, flee, as if the devil himself were in pursuit, from sects and fanatics, like the Pope, the Sacramentarians and others, who try to substitute human notions for the written Word. If we yield to such as these, we step, as it were, from the rock into the quicksand, where, the more we try to gain a foot-hold, the more we sink, and where it is impossible to save ourselves. God's Word alone is the true and enduring rock that affords a sure foundation. Let him, therefore, who would walk in the right way, see that he has God's Word. When Christ says, "This is my body," "this is my blood," let him believe and not follow the deceivers who say, It is mere bread, it is mere wine. When Christ says, "He that believeth on me shall never see death," let him believe it and not obey the Pope, who points him to the sacrifice of the mass, to the intercession of saints and to good works. Then he may be sure that he is right, and that he has escaped the offence.

We now propose briefly to consider also the second point, viz.: why it was decreed in God's especial counsel that God's Son, our Lord and Saviour, should die just as He did; for the Jews held the death upon the cross as the most offensive and disgraceful, and as far more detestable than we hold the death upon the gallows or the wheel. We find the reason for this written Deut. 21: "And if a man have committed a sin worthy of death, and he be to be put to death, and thou hang him on a tree, his body shall not remain all night upon the tree, but thou shalt in any wise bury him that day; (for he that is hanged is accursed of God;) that thy land be not defiled, which the Lord thy God giveth thee for an inheritance."

Now, it is indifferent whether God pronounces this severe judgment upon those hanged in view of the future calamity that His Son Himself should be thus slain, or in view of the past calamity that disobedient man fell in Paradise and ate of the forbidden fruit. The chief and most important consideration here is, that we should learn and remember well that God calls all those accursed who die on the tree. For from this it immediately follows that, since Christ also died on a tree, He too became a curse and was called accursed. Hence the devil and the world took particular delight in bringing upon Him that very death which God Himself had called accursed. Paul, however, teaches us how we must understand this passage in Deut., and whether its contents ought to be a subject for joy or for offence; for in speaking of it he says, Gal. 3:

"Christ hath redeemed us from the curse of the law, being made a curse for us; for it is written, Cursed is every one that hangeth on a tree; that the blessing of Abraham might come on the Gentiles through Jesus Christ; that we might receive the promise of the Spirit through faith."

We should, by all means, consider this passage carefully. Paul very nicely brings the two little words, "curse" and "blessing," side by side, and leads us back to the promise made to Abraham when God said, "In thy seed shall all the nations of the earth be blessed." For it follows that, if in Abraham's seed all the nations of the earth were to be blessed, all the nations of the earth must have been under the curse; else they would not have needed a promise of blessing. Again, this seed, in which the blessing was to come, must have been that only blessed seed, with which God is not wroth, but which He accompanies with pure grace and blessing. It is plain, however, who this seed of Abraham is; namely, Jesus Christ, born of the virgin Mary, the Only Begotten of the Father, and the only one full of grace and truth. All others, counting from Adam to the very last man, are not children of grace by nature, but God is angry with them and hostile to them, and they are not blessed, but cursed. And why? Because they all are sinners.

But behold the result! The blessed seed of Abraham is nailed to that tree, or cross, to which God refers when He says, "Cursed is every one that hangeth on a tree;" and it is therefore no longer called the blessed seed, but the accursed. Paul comes out boldly with this, saying, Christ was "made a curse." Let us hear the reason for this.

It is we who, on account of our sins, are a curse, and under the wrath of God. Christ, the only begotten Son of God, is full of grace and truth. How, then, does He come to be nailed to the tree? Why does He thrust Himself under the wrath of God? It was for our sake, Paul tells us; "He was made a curse for us;" He desired to bear God's wrath and atone for our sins, that we might be made blessed, that is, receive the Holy Spirit, be freed from sin, and become the children of God. This may be illustrated by the case of a poor beggar who has many debts, but is unable to pay them; another man, who is able to pay these debts, comes to his assistance, becomes his surety, thus making himself a debtor, and pays the poor man's debts. Paul expresses this very nicely, Rom. 8: "The law could not" deliver us from sin and death, and so God Himself helped us. He sent "His own Son in the likeness of sinful flesh," that is, His Son became man, assuming our flesh and blood. And God "for sin, condemned sin in the flesh," that is, God has made us free from sin through His only begotten Son, who became a sin-offering and had to atone for sin, thus bringing the blessing of Abraham upon us who were under the curse. In 2 Cor. 5, Paul himself interprets this latter: God "hath made Him to be sin for us, who knew no sin; that we might be made the righteousness of God in Him."

Christ, therefore, became both "a curse," and afterward also "sin," that is, a sin-offering, upon which rest the sins of all men, and hence also the wrath of God and a miserable death. Since these things rest upon this offering, we are relieved, for they rest on us no longer. This is the reason why John the Baptist calls Him a Lamb, meaning a sheep for the slaughter, a Sacrifice, appointed by God to take away the sins of the whole world. And the Lord Himself says, John 12: "And I, if I be lifted up from the earth, will draw all men unto me." And again, John 3: "As Moses lifted up the serpent in the wilderness, even so must the Son of man be lifted up; that whosoever believeth in Him should not perish, but have everlasting life."

Paul says that he did not know anything and was "determined not to know anything," "save Jesus Christ, and Him crucified." Christ was crucified so that He might sanctify, deliver and justify us, who, had we been left to ourselves, would have eternally remained and perished under sin and death, and under the tyranny of Satan.

And should we now be offended at the cross? Was it, after all, an ignominious death? We should heartily thank God that His Son hangs upon the cross, bearing the curse under which we should still be on account of our sins. There He hangs as one condemned, and as one whom God hates and visits now with shame and want and agony. This is so, Paul says, for thy sake and for my sake, that the blessing might come on us. For if the curse had continued to rest on us, we would never have received the blessing. But lo, the blessed Seed draws near and takes the curse, which rests on us, upon Himself, and the blessing, which rests on Him, He gives to us. Since He would and should become a curse for us, no other death except this death on the cross was suitable, for this is the death which God's Word had declared accursed.

Let us, then, thoroughly learn here to judge, not according to what the eye perceives, but according to what the Word of God declares. According to appearances the Lord Jesus' death is a shameful death and, as God Himself calls it, an accursed death; and the tree on which He dies, an execrable tree,—a cursed cross, and this because all our sins hang on it. For sin and the curse, or God's anger, and every misfortune,—all these belong together. Therefore Isaiah says: "Many were astonished at Thee; His visage was so marred more than any man, and His form more than the sons of men." Again: "When we shall see Him, there is no beauty that we should desire Him. He is despised and rejected of men; a man of sorrows, and acquainted with grief: and we hid as it were our faces from Him; He was despised, and we esteemed Him not." This is the way these things appear, and it is impossible for human reason to see them in a different light, because God calls everyone accursed who dies on a tree. The cross is cursed; He who hangs on it is cursed; the cause of His hanging there is also cursed, for sin demands the curse; and the greater the number of sins that lie on the Lord Jesus, the greater also the curse.

But let us look a little further and find what follows from this that Christ, the blessed Seed, dies such an accursed death and becomes a curse for us Himself. Paul, in very appropriate words, states this as the result: "That the blessing of Abraham might come on the Gentiles," and that thus "we might receive the Holy Spirit." This we find to be altogether different from that which we can see with the bodily eye. This disgraceful death which God has cursed is an offence to the eye, but to us it is a blessed death, for it takes the curse away from us and brings God's blessing to us. The tree which in itself is an accursed tree, is for us a blissful tree. It is that precious altar, upon which God's Son offers Himself to God, His Father, for our sins. It is that glorious altar, at which He appears as the true and eternal priest. For He is brought to the tree, and He makes it a blessed altar, that we might be released from sin, and receive God's grace and be God's children.

No wonder, then, that the old teachers entertained such excellent thoughts about the cross and the accursed tree. There in Paradise, they say, a beautiful tree occasioned our falling into sin and death; here, however, an old, dry, yes accursed tree occasioned our deliverance from sin and our receiving everlasting life. Here hangs God's Son with arms extended as a testimony that He will cast no one out, but gladly receive everyone and draw all unto Him, as He says He will, John 12. His head is lifted toward heaven, pointing out to us the way of life eternal. His feet reach toward the ground where they bruise the head of Satan, that old serpent creeping on the earth, forcing from him all his power. That power over us which Satan received because of our sins he surely loses now, in virtue of the dear Lord Jesus' hanging on the cross, where He atones for our sins with His death and becomes a curse in our stead.

Therefore, let us here learn to acknowledge and to praise our merciful heavenly Father's gracious will toward us. For He spared not His own Son, but delivered Him up to die, yea, to die upon the cross, and suffered Him to be made a curse; so that we might obtain the blessing, be set free from sin, receive the Holy Spirit, and through Him become God's children and be eternally saved. God grant this to us all. Amen.

11

Christ's Prayer on the Cross.— The Malefactor on the Right

Two other men, both criminals, were also led out with him to be executed. When they came to the place called the Skull, they crucified him there, along with the criminals—one on his right, the other on his left. Jesus said, "Father, forgive them, for they do not know what they are doing." And they divided up his clothes by casting lots. The people stood watching, and the rulers even sneered at him. They said, "He saved others; let him save himself if he is God's Messiah, the Chosen One." The soldiers also came up and mocked him. They offered him wine vinegar and said, "If you are the king of the Jews, save yourself." There was a written notice above him, which read: this is the king of the jews. One of the criminals who hung there hurled insults at him: "Aren't you the Messiah? Save yourself and us!" But the other criminal rebuked him. "Don't you fear God," he said, "since you are under the same sentence? We are punished justly, for we are getting what our deeds deserve. But this man has done nothing wrong." Then he said, "Jesus, remember me when you come into your kingdom." Jesus answered him, "Truly I tell you, today you will be with me in paradise."

—LUKE 23:32–43

The holy Evangelist here mentions two things that are very consolatory. Therefore, although the other Evangelists have omitted them in their record of Christ's sufferings, we shall treat of them here, so that this record may be before us in its completeness. The first of these things is, that Christ, immediately after the cross, to which He had been nailed, was erected, began to pray, saying, "Father, forgive them; for they know not what they do." The other thing we wish to notice is, that the malefactor on the right of Christ, hearing this prayer, learned from it that Jesus was the Son of God and the very Christ, and therefore desired to be remembered by Him when He should have come into His kingdom.

Let us now consider these two things, for they are full of consolation and we can never sufficiently meditate upon them nor explain them. And, besides all this, it is necessary for us, not only to behold the works and sufferings of this Man, but also most carefully to heed the words proclaimed by Him; for these declare the reason of His deeds and sufferings, and their consequence.

It is of the greatest importance, however, to distinguish between the suffering of our Lord Jesus and that of all other men. This distinction is momentous, not only because Jesus Christ is eternal God, who created heaven and earth and all things, but also because His suffering had a peculiar cause, and because the benefit, or fruit, of His suffering is such that it could not have been produced by the suffering of any other man, or of an angel, or of any creature. He suffered, as you lately heard, not for Himself, but for us, that we might be delivered from sin and death. This we also learn from the words He here speaks in our text, which words it behooves every Christian to observe and to entwine in his soul as his most precious treasure and comfort.

The words He spoke upon the cross, "Father, forgive them; for they know not what they do," clearly show, that He was attending to His true priestly office even while suspended in the air upon the cross; and that He was fulfilling the work which brought Him to earth, not only with His suffering, in that He sacrificed Himself, but also with prayer, both sacrifice and prayer belonging to the office of the priest. Christ tells us that the sacrifice consisted chiefly in His sanctifying Himself for our sakes, so that we "also might be sanctified through the truth," John 17; or, according to John 10, in His laying down His "life for the sheep." There are many more passages of this kind, all of which show that His sufferings were not to be for Himself, but for us. The zeal with which He here performed this work and offered this sacrifice was such that He even prayed that the Father would forgive those who crucified Him,—that He would pardon and not punish their sin. He prayed thus that all might know why He was brought to the cross, and that they might receive comfort from this knowledge.

This prayer, therefore, should teach us, first of all, that our dear Lord Jesus is a priest, and that He fulfilled the duties of His priestly office there upon the cross. To pray for sinners is, indeed, one of the proper employments of the priesthood. Now, Aaron, serving under the law, was invested with peculiar priestly apparel made for glory and for beauty. But would we know with what priestly robes Christ was clad and what the altar was at which He served, we need merely look at the cross. There we see Him entirely naked, full of wounds and void of every trace of sacerdotal splendor. Still He attended to His priestly duties most perfectly and carefully, even praying for His foes. Let us not be offended at His unpriestly appearance, for the work of this Priest has a significance entirely different from that of Moses' priests. This difference we learn even from the superscription written over Him, which declares Him to be "The King of the Jews," the correctness of which title He had Himself publicly and clearly confessed before Pilate.

Neither does this title harmonize with His appearance. Instead of wearing a scarlet robe, His body is covered with blood and wounds and bruises. Instead of a golden crown, He wears a crown of thorns. There upon the cross we see a Priest and King, of whom the world is ashamed, whom the world despises, and whom it regards as neither King nor Priest. This is just what Isaiah says: "When we shall see Him, there is no beauty that we should desire Him. He is despised and rejected of men; a man of sorrows and acquainted with grief: and we hid as it were our faces from Him; He was despised, and we esteemed Him not." This Priest offers us His own body and blood upon the cross in a place that was dishonored, desecrated, yea, accursed. This shall ever be our dearest, loveliest and most graceful garment, no matter how it is regarded by the world and the natural eye. Bulls, heifers and calves were sacrificed in the temple upon a consecrated altar, but Christ sacrifices Himself upon an altar that was not consecrated. Gallows and places of execution are to this day horrid and dishonorable, and Moses writes: "He that is hanged is accursed of God." Now, the world thinks it disgraceful and dishonorable that this Priest was not permitted to bring His offering even to the place where heifers and calves were sacrificed. But this was for us and for our good, that we might learn that He has brought a fully satisfactory offering for our sins, as it was stated already in the preceding sermon. Since our sins could not be atoned for and removed by any other than this Priest who is the eternal Son of God, it is our fault that He could not have a more honorable altar and a more precious garment. This is no hindrance, however, to the discharge of His office. He not only does offer His body and blood, but also prays for poor, ignorant sinners.

We should, therefore, be heartily comforted because of this Priest and His office. Even as He suffers not alone for those who were present at His crucifixion, took hold of Him and nailed Him to the cross, so neither does He pray for them alone, but also for us, otherwise the prayer of Christ would receive too limited an interpretation. Those present then were merely our servants and ministers. Had it not been my sin and thy sin that nailed the Lord Jesus to the cross, these men would surely not have been able to molest Him.

He now comes forward as the true High Priest and Lamb of God, by the sacrifice of Himself to atone for the sins of all the world and to conquer death for men, and this is the only reason why the Jews and Gentiles receive power to harm Him. Thus we see that when He prays for those who crucify Him, He prays for us and all men, who by our sins had furnished the cause for His crucifixion and death. For this reason we should not regard the gallows, or the cross, on which Christ suffered, as anything else than that altar, upon which He offers up His life and at which He discharges the priestly duty of prayer, to the end that we might be free from sin and everlasting death. For whoever takes sin away, takes away death also, because when sin is gone then death has lost its power, and therefore hell also.

Christ, our only and eternal High Priest, is the One who has done this for us on the cross. He has reconciled us to God, without the intervention of our works, by His own sufferings, having been made a curse for us, having died upon the cross for our sins, and having finally prayed for sinners. Let us, therefore, not forget heartily to thank Him for this.

True, even popery preaches on this theme. But, although the text tells us so clearly and the history relates to us so plainly that Christ sacrificed Himself upon the cross for our benefit, and that He suffered in our stead, popery uses many words to make the populace believe that men must be their own priests, that they themselves must sacrifice for sin, and that their own works must merit life eternal. Therefore, when we now teach, and God be praised that we do teach it, that the Evangelists plainly write that Christ, the true and eternal High Priest, has delivered us from death and obtained everlasting life for us by the sacrifice of Himself, the blind and wretched hirelings of the Pope curse and condemn the divine truth and call it scandalous heresy. Terrible and woeful anger, blindness and punishment has surely been poured out upon the ungrateful world in that the blasphemers, these Papists, themselves confess and preach that Christ offered Himself on the cross for us, and, at the same time, rage against us and shed innocent blood because we teach this doctrine and point the people to this sure and everlasting consolation. Truly, this is a realization of Isaiah's denunciation against the despisers of God's Word: "Hear ye indeed, but understand not; and see ye indeed, but perceive not," and receive ye a hardened and foolish heart. If this were not the case it would be inexplicable why they so lightly esteem this Sacrifice and place all their confidence in their own, man-appointed works, such as cities, garments and food, "which all," Paul says, "are to perish with the using." O, why will men not take the consolation offered here, viz., that Christ sacrificed His body and His life and, praying for us, said: Father, here am I, a Mediator between Thee and poor sinners; I die for them; I give myself for them; be gracious unto them.

Notwithstanding that our adversaries themselves read, confess and preach this, they will continue to yell and foam at it and to condemn us as heretics. Well, this is the visitation of God's dreadful wrath upon them. May the Lord in mercy shield us against such visitation. But should He ever suffer us to fall, I pray that He would let us fall into a sin which we may feel and acknowledge, and not into one that bids direct defiance to His grace and that is looked upon as holiness, whose outward features it assumes.

Let us, therefore, open our hearts and behold Christ, our High Priest, in His proper priestly garment and at His proper priestly work. The eye does not see Him arrayed in beauty or in wealth, but finds Him ignominiously hanging there in misery and wretchedness. But if we look into His heart we shall discover ornaments so bright and treasures so rich that we can never thank Him for them sufficiently. He is adorned, in the first place, with that most sincere obedience in which He glorifies His Father by permitting Himself to be spit upon, scourged and tortured. In this life we cannot fully comprehend the glory of this ornament; still we can understand enough of it to know that all pearls and purple and gold are nothing beside it. His other ornament is that great love He has for us which makes Him care so little about His life and His sufferings, almost forgetting them in the heartfelt interest He takes in our condition and in our need, and praying for us rather than for Himself. We cannot sufficiently understand such love as this; for in the heart of the Lord there is burning such a flame of love for us, that He does not seem to see or to feel His own most severe suffering, torture and disgrace, but only considers and perceives and cares for thy and my misery, distress and affliction.

We cannot help acknowledging that the love of the Lord, who is so concerned about us that He entirely overlooks His own danger, injury and pain, is indeed a mighty, burning love. Father and mother, when their dear child is in danger or want, rush through the fire to save it, caring not for their own safety, but only for that of their child. The love of our Lord Jesus is also such that He passes through affliction as through a fire, to grasp us with the hand of mercy and affection. Now, this is the fitting garment with which our eternal High Priest is arrayed. This is not an outer vestment for the eye of reason to behold; but the eye of faith perceives it in Jesus within, as His words also sufficiently testify.

The chief thing in the entire history of the passion is that Christ gave Himself for us and, caring for nothing as much as for our deliverance, reached toward us, and pursued us through all manner of affliction as through a fire. To this main point we should pay especial attention, and cling to it so closely that it cannot be wrested from our hands.

We have need of this doctrine not only as a source of comfort, but also as a source of strength, with which to counteract the poison prescribed to the people by the Pope, who would lift them into heaven by their own righteousness and work and merit. If our works could have done this, why was it necessary for Christ, the Son of God, to suffer? But here we find Him obediently and patiently bringing His offering, His own body and life, and beseeching His Father to have mercy and to forgive. This is proof enough that nothing of the kind could have been accomplished with our works; for it is not as easy a thing to obtain forgiveness of sins as the Papists dream. True, it is easy enough to put on a cowl and to fast, keep vigils and sing a great deal; but to come into possession of pardon for sin requires something quite different from our filthy works, and something far greater. If we rely on our fasts and vigils and prayers, we will have to wait quite a while indeed to receive help of God! But Isaiah states the plan: "He was wounded for our transgressions, He was bruised for our iniquities;" "He hath borne our griefs." The Papists themselves are constrained to confess that the sufferings and death of the Lord Jesus are far exalted above our prayers, our good works, our sufferings, our charity, our fasting. He, therefore, who tries to atone for sin with such things as these, shall surely not succeed. To succeed in this requires, as Isaiah clearly says, a different man and different works and merits. Therefore, he who would apply his own merits to the removing of sin, blasphemes the death and sacrifice and prayer of Christ, because he makes his own prayer and offering equal, nay, superior, to the offering and prayer of Christ. Against this abomination we must diligently guard.

The Lord does not however, pray at random, but makes a distinction between those for whom He prays and others, saying, "Father, forgive them; for they know not what they do." He thus designates two classes of sinners. Some know that they do wrong, and still do so without fear, prompted by pure malice and hatred against the acknowledged divine truth. These commit the "sin unto death," as it is called 1 John 5, that is, the sin against the Holy Ghost, if they continue in such willful sin and do not confess, abstain from and ask forgiveness for it, but remain impenitent to the end, and besides blaspheme the Word of God and the truth which cannot be gainsaid, as most of the Papists now are doing.

The Papists know that our doctrine is true and divine; they know that Christ commanded us to receive the whole Sacrament, that He did not forbid matrimony, that He gave no command concerning the sacrifice of the mass, and that He died for our sins. Still, they condemn us, who hold these doctrines, as heretics, and punish those of their subjects whom they discover believing our doctrine and using the Sacrament as it was instituted by Christ. This is willful persecution of the truth, and therefore not a sin of ignorance. They commit this sin in such a way that it cannot be forgiven them; for it is a sin that is in direct conflict with forgiveness, because it is neither abandoned nor confessed. Forgiveness of sin demands that sin be both confessed and renounced.

Other sinners sin ignorantly. But we must understand their case correctly. David, for instance, knew well enough that he was doing wrong and sinning against God in taking the wife of Uriah and then having him slain. But his carnal lust and the devil so impetuously impelled him to the deed that he committed it before rightly considering what he was doing. Afterward, however, he confessed his sin, was grieved by it, wished that he had not committed it, and prayed for mercy.

We all are encumbered with this sin and are easily and unawares led astray. Sometimes we fall through fear, sometimes through carelessness and weakness, like Peter, and sometimes through presumptuousness. Such sins Christ bore with Him to the cross and for such He prayed; for these are bare and naked sins, which are not inconsistent with grace, being recognized and confessed and their forgiveness being sought. Thus we often find that harlots, villains, murderers, and other wicked people, who know that they have done wrong and make no attempt at justifying themselves, find mercy. To the believer God does not impute such acknowledged sins, because the sacrifice of Christ is interposed between them and God. But they who knowingly and willfully persist in sin and even excuse their sins, sin against the Holy Ghost and deny the grace of God. For them Christ does not pray here, but only for those who know not what they do, and who, as said before, fall through fear, weakness and the like. The latter can rely upon the offering and prayer of Christ and can be assured that their sins are forgiven, for Christ here prays for them, and His prayer was surely accepted. We must not doubt this, but find in it consolation and joy.

So much it was meet briefly to say concerning Christ's prayer on the cross, with which He declares why He is suffering there, namely, that they who sin ignorantly and then repent might, for His sake, have a merciful God, who does not impute to them, but graciously forgives, their sin.

Let us now look a little also at the history of the malefactor on the right of Christ. We can nowhere find an incident of more remarkable beauty than here. The poor fellow cannot deny his sins; he knows that he has sinned, and that he must now die for his sins. He cannot, therefore, boast before God of any good works, or of any merit of his own. He even reproves his comrade, who, railing on the Lord Jesus, said, "If Thou be Christ, save Thyself and us," by answering him thus: We are indeed justly punished, "for we receive the due reward of our deeds: but this Man hath done nothing amiss." He thus confesses that he had well deserved that dreadful death. It is a matter of astonishment, therefore, in the first place, that, having every reason to fear God on account of his sins, the malefactor still was confident, as we shall hear, that the Lord Jesus would take him with Him into His kingdom.

It is a matter of great astonishment, in the second place, that this one man did not stumble at the huge stumbling-stone laid in his way by the entire council of Jerusalem, including the temporal and spiritual government, which mocked and reviled the Lord Jesus. The chief spiritual rulers said: "He saved others, let Him save Himself, if He be Christ, the Chosen of God." The soldiers also mocked Him, saying, "If Thou be the King of the Jews, save Thyself;" for the superscription written over Him declared that He was "Jesus of Nazareth, the King of the Jews." The malefactor crucified on the left of Christ said: "If Thou be Christ, save Thyself and us." This he said, not because he desired help, but because he wanted to insult and ridicule the Lord. In short, the whole world is offended in Christ, who hangs on the cross, and it does not esteem Him. Even the disciples, although a part of them stood by the cross, had lost all hope.

The poor malefactor on the right alone steps over the rock of offence and dares to call Christ, who hangs on the cross at his side, a Lord and King. He gives the lie to all the world, cares not what others think of him, and proclaims Christ to be an everlasting King. These are his words: "Lord, remember me when Thou comest into Thy kingdom." He calls Christ a Lord, says He has a kingdom, and desires Him, when He shall have entered His kingdom, to remember him. Now, the time rendered it certain, that neither of them could live till evening. Therefore he believes that Christ is the Lord of another and an eternal life. This faith and this confession, found, as it was, in the midst of a world that despaired of Christ and hated Him, must have been indeed a great and exquisite faith,—a glorious confession.

The question may occur to us, whence could the malefactor have obtained this abundant and accurate knowledge, by which he was able to recognize and proclaim Christ as the Lord of eternal life, or who could have been his instructor? Without a doubt, he learned this alone from Christ's prayer on the cross. The prophet Isaiah, chap. 53, declares that the Messiah should suffer and be "numbered with the transgressors," and also that He should bear "the sins of many and make intercession for the transgressors." This prophecy was fulfilled on the cross. The innocent Lord, who had done no evil, hangs there between two murderers. And as He begins to pray, and says, "Father, forgive them; for they know not what they do," the malefactor catches the little word "Father." People were not in the habit of conversing with God in this way. Christ is the only One who can speak thus to God, and He it is who has taught us thus to speak. The malefactor hence concludes that Christ must be God's Son, and recognizes Him, by His praying for sinners, as the true Messiah, or Christ. The quoted passages from Isaiah, and similar passages from other prophets which he had heard, either in the temple at Jerusalem, or elsewhere in some synagogue, but which he had not understood, now, no doubt, occurred to him. He takes these passages together, and the Holy Spirit makes these prophecies so bright and clear to his soul that he can contain himself no longer, but confesses with his lips what he believes in his heart, and says, "Lord, remember me when Thou comest into Thy kingdom."

He would say: Thou art the Son of God. For our sins Thou sufferest on earth this dreadful death upon the cross. But Thou shalt afterward ascend into an everlasting kingdom and be Lord over all. There, O Lord, remember me! I am willing now to die, for I have well deserved death. But do Thou not forget me when Thou comest into Thy kingdom.—Behold, what a deep knowledge of Christ Jesus this man derived from Christ's short prayer! This prayer was the sermon that taught him true wisdom.

The knowledge and confession of Christ which proceeded from the malefactor on the cross, is the very same knowledge and confession by which God preserves the Christian Church to-day. Though everything else should fail, and emperors, kings, popes and bishops cease to be, God will still retain a small company that shall have His Spirit and that shall confess His name before the world. When the disciples, and others who are closely allied to the Lord Jesus, refuse to confess and believe, and deny the Lord through fear, and are offended in Him and desert Him, then some malefactor or murderer must appear, to confess this Christ, to preach concerning Him, and to teach others what they should think of Him and why they should be comforted in Him. The Lord our God is determined not to leave Christ without followers who confess Him, even if He must have recourse to the thief upon the gallows, or the murderer upon the wheel.

This is, therefore, a consoling history; for it teaches us, first of all, that they who follow Christ and receive all mercy from Him, are none other than those sinners who confess their sins and heartily pray for grace; these shall receive grace and mercy. With His previous prayer, "Father, forgive them," &c., His present action corresponds; He suffers now, that sin may be forgiven. And then, upon the cross, before He dies, the dear Lord soon proves, in the case of the malefactor, or murderer, how beneficial and powerful His sufferings are and what they avail. He there proves that His sufferings benefit all poor sinners who, with the malefactor, believe and confess that Christ is an eternal King; that by His agony, death and resurrection He has acquired for them the forgiveness of their sins and their deliverance from everlasting death; and that He will take them into His eternal kingdom.

Hence we can conclude with such certainty as not to entertain the vestige of a doubt, that Christ did not offer Himself on the cross for saints, for no mortal, let him be who he may, is holy of himself; but that He offered Himself for sinners, for He came to call sinners to repentance and not the righteous, as He Himself says, Matt. 9. Therefore, he who tries to get to heaven by means of a holy life, good works, and personal merits, deceives himself. He who does not confess himself a sinner, can find no access to the Lord Jesus; for Christ did not die for His own, but for the sinner's sake.

Christ converted the malefactor on the cross into a saint, not suffering him to remain and to perish in his sins. We should therefore regard this history as an example showing by very deed what the Redeemer sought and acquired by His sufferings, and what He accomplished by the priestly sacrifice and prayer which He offered on the cross. He took sin upon Himself, not because He delights in sin, neither because He would have us remain under sin and continue in iniquity. No, He suffers for sinners so that they need not go on in sin, and so that they may become converted and be pious and holy. This His purpose was accomplished in the case of the malefactor, who, being converted, accused himself of sin, but still trusted in the Lord Jesus, believing that God, through Him and for His sake, would forgive his sins and give him life eternal.

The malefactor is thus made an entirely different man. His shameful and justly merited death now becomes a real act of divine service. He suffers no longer as a murderer, but as a saint. He dies in the true confession and in heart-felt confidence in God's grace through Christ. He is sincerely grieved for his sins. He now begins to obey God and to do many good works. With his sufferings he honors and praises God. Publicly, before all the world, he glorifies the crucified Jesus, exhorting and admonishing everyone to repent and to believe in this Lord. In short, his faith in Christ does not only cause him to be a saint, but it even bears him into paradise and into everlasting life, according to Christ's promise: "To-day shalt thou be with me in paradise."

Let us follow this example and not act like the rude and ungodly, who say: I will sin so that Christ may have a chance to save me and to show me mercy. No, no; but let us say: I am born in sin and am full of filth and evil lusts. It is, therefore, not necessary for me first to sin in order to be able to confess myself a sinner. I have, alas, been only too great a sinner from the very beginning! I am already under the curse of God and condemned to eternal death. Therefore, since God in infinite compassion calls me to repentance, will I now turn myself unto Him and take refuge in this Lord, whose suffering has ransomed sinners, and whose innocent death has delivered me from the death so well deserved and long since merited, and who has reconciled me unto God!

He, however, who abuses this sermon of mercy, and refuses to forsake and confess and repent of his sins, may look upon the murderer on the left of Christ and upon the rulers of the Jews and upon the soldiers, and consider how they fared in their wickedness and what they merited with their impenitent lives. If we would be benefited by the Lord Jesus and by His agony and prayer, we must follow the example of the malefactor who confessed his sins and prayed for grace, and acknowledged that Christ was the Lord and the King of everlasting life. May the dear Lord Jesus, our eternal King, grant us this. Amen.

12

Christ Commits His Mother to the Care of John.— The Soldiers do not Break the Legs of Christ, but with a Spear Pierce His Side, from which Blood and Water Flow

Near the cross of Jesus stood his mother, his mother's sister, Mary the wife of Clopas, and Mary Magdalene. When Jesus saw his mother there, and the disciple whom he loved standing nearby, he said to her, "Woman, here is your son," and to the disciple, "Here is your mother." From that time on, this disciple took her into his home. Later, knowing that everything had now been finished, and so that Scripture would be fulfilled, Jesus said, "I am thirsty." A jar of wine vinegar was there, so they soaked a sponge in it, put the sponge on a stalk of the hyssop plant, and lifted it to Jesus' lips. When he had received the drink, Jesus said, "It is finished." With that, he bowed his head and gave up his spirit. Now it was the day of Preparation, and the next day was to be a special Sabbath. Because the Jewish leaders did not want the bodies left on the crosses during the Sabbath, they asked Pilate to have the legs broken and the bodies taken down. The soldiers therefore came and broke the legs of the first man who had been crucified with Jesus, and then those of the other. But when they came to Jesus and found that he was already dead, they did not break his legs. Instead, one of the soldiers pierced Jesus' side with a spear, bringing a sudden flow of blood and water. The man who saw it has given testimony, and his testimony is true. He knows that he tells the truth, and he testifies so that you also may believe. These things happened so that the scripture would be fulfilled: "Not one of his bones will be broken," and, as another scripture says, "They will look on the one they have pierced."

—**JOHN 19:25–37**

St. John, toward the end of the passion history, relates three things, about which the other Evangelists do not write, but which are, nevertheless, very important in point of doctrine and consolation. These also must be considered, that we may have the whole of this history before us.

The first of these things is, that Christ, while on the cross, commends His mother to John, and also John to His mother, so that they might be inclined toward each other as are a mother and her son, and that they might love and in every way assist each other. John tells us too that he immediately took the mother of Jesus into his care and treated her as if she had been his own mother.

This narrative is generally regarded as an illustration of the fourth commandment, which says: "Honor thy father and thy mother, that thy days may be long upon the land which the Lord thy God giveth thee." With this accords the fact that John lived longer than the rest of the Apostles, namely, sixty-eight years after the resurrection. Although this explanation is not improper as far as it goes, it is still too narrow; for that which the Lord does and says here upon the cross dare not be regarded as done and said for only a few individuals. Christ intended His works and words to embrace the whole world, but especially the Christian Church.

That, therefore, which Christ here says to Mary and John alone, we must regard as a command for all Christians and for the entire Church. Since Christ hangs upon the cross and, by His death, saves us all from sin and death, we must be toward each other like a mother and her son, who in all things sincerely love, aid and advise each other. This is the meaning also of the command which the Lord so often repeats during the last Supper: "This is my commandment, that ye love one another, as I have loved you;" "A new commandment I give unto you, That ye love one another, as I have loved you." The love between a mother and her children is the deepest and most sincere that can be found.

The Lord uses the words "mother" and "son" with special reference to both parts of the Church, viz., to those who teach the Word and to those who hear. Even as a mother nourishes her infant and diligently cares for it till it is grown up and has become strong, so honest pastors also labor and take pains to teach the people and render them good Christians. Thus Paul calls his disciples, whom he had reared as with a mother's trouble and toil, children, 1 Cor. 4; Gal. 4; 1 Thess. 2. The Church cannot be properly conducted unless they who exercise the office of the ministry have for her the affection of a mother. If they have not this love, the result will be indolence, indifference and unwillingness to suffer. The Lord very explicitly teaches this in the 21. chapter of John. He there commands Peter to preach, but not until He had three times asked him: "Simon, son of Jonas, lovest thou me?" By this question He meant to say: Unless thou lovest the lambs as a mother loves her children, whom she tries to rescue from the flames even at the peril of her own life, thou wilt never be fit for a preacher. In thy office as pastor, trouble, toil, ingratitude, hatred, envy and many a cross will be thy lot. Now, if the pastors have no motherly heart, no fervent love for the flock, these shall receive poor care indeed.

On the other hand, again, they who have not received the command to preach, but stand in need of information and instruction, must deport themselves like sons, suffering themselves to be taught, led, nourished, and cared for in other ways, thus conducting themselves toward their teachers as a pious child conducts itself toward its mother. True, children's love for their mother is not as great as the mother's love for her children, even as the proverb says: *Amor descendit, non ascendit*, that is, love moves downward, not upward. Still, nature prompts pious children to honor their parents, and to serve them and yield to them in everything that they desire and need. When this is the relation between mother and son, between pastor and congregation, then all is well.

If, however, the ministers of the Church are lacking in motherly affection, or if the hearers are void of childlike fidelity, it is out of the question that things should go right and that God should be pleased. This we have sadly experienced in the case of the Pope, the bishops and the whole priestly rabble, for they have no such motherly love. They think that the office was given them merely that they might be great lords and live at their ease. Therefore, they not only take poor care of the sheep, but they even, to their heart's content, skin and butcher the lambs in life, property and soul, as we only too well see. Again, we frequently find the deficiency in the hearers, that they, like ill-bred children, do not properly provide for their pastors. This is the case, among us, with peasants, with citizens, and especially with the nobility, who deal so closely, stingily and niggardly with their pastors, that seldom one is found who willingly gives to the ministry as much as he should. And this is done in spite of St. Paul's pointed and earnest admonition, not to communicate sparingly of our carnal things unto them that communicate unto us spiritual things. Such ingratitude cannot fail to injure the cause of the Gospel, neither can God's punishment fail to come upon such perverse children.

We should, therefore, carefully observe and take to heart this command of our Lord Jesus, who, upon the cross, shows such tender solicitude both for the teacher and the disciple, that is, for the whole Church. Teachers and pastors He exhorts to motherly love, and pulpits and congregations to childlike faithfulness, gratitude and obedience. If both parties obey these blessed instructions of our dear Lord Jesus, all will be well and God will bless and give success. So much for the first point.

The other two points, that no bone of Christ was broken and that His side was pierced with a spear, do not appear to be of much importance. Since, however, the Evangelist John adduces the clear testimony of the Scriptures, that Moses and Zechariah had prophesied these things many centuries before they took place, and since the Holy Spirit speaks nothing that is useless or vain, we are bound to confess that these two facts are of great moment, however much they may have the appearance of trifles. The holy Evangelist John, according to true apostolic custom, confers on us a special blessing by everywhere quoting and interpreting Scripture so appropriately.

Moses, as we have already heard, wrote the clear command that no one should "remain all night upon the tree," for God had said that this would defile the land. As this was the day for the preparation, and as the Sabbath would begin with the setting of the sun, the Jews besought Pilate to have the bodies removed from the cross, so that they might be buried yet by day, before the beginning of the festival. Pilate gave his consent. But as they found the two malefactors yet living, the soldiers, as John says, hastened their departure, at the command of the Jews, by breaking their arms and legs, as they were hanging on the cross. They intended to do the same with the Lord Jesus, but He gave up the ghost before they had finished with the two malefactors, and therefore "they brake not His legs. But one of the soldiers with a spear pierced His side," from which, to the astonishment of all, both blood and water flowed. These two things, as I have said, seem of little importance, but John testifies that they were not mere accidents, but that both of them had been foretold, the one by Moses, "Neither shall ye break a bone," the other by Zechariah, "They shall look upon me whom they have pierced."

Now, it is true, indeed, that what Moses says, Ex. 12 and Num. 9, refers to the passover. How, then, could it occur to the Evangelist John to say: "These things were done that the Scripture should be fulfilled, A bone of Him shall not be broken," and what does he mean by this? He would simply teach us to look upon the Lord Jesus on the cross as the true Passover, of which the old passover in the law is merely the type or symbol.

When God desired with violence to weaken the might of Pharaoh in Egypt and to frustrate his obstinate wantonness and design, and to save His people Israel, He commanded His people, the Jews, in each house, in the appointed night, to slay a lamb of the first year and roast and eat it, but to strike its blood on the door-posts. The destroying angel was to pass over that house on whose doors he should see the token of the blood and smite none of its inmates. But where the token of the lamb's blood on the door was wanting, there the angel was in that night to smite throughout all Egypt the first-born both of man and beast. As Moses had told the people at God's command, so it came to pass. In the morning dead men and beasts were found in the houses of all the Egyptians, the destroyer having spared the Jews alone, because their doors were marked and protected by the blood of the lamb.

Let us now turn to our Paschal Lamb, Christ Jesus. He desires to punish Pharaoh and all Egypt, that is, sin, death and Satan, and to rescue His Christian Church from tyranny. Therefore He suffers Himself to be slain like the lamb of old, and to be sacrificed upon the cross, so that He might sprinkle us with His blood, and so that the destroying angel, who, on account of our sins, had brought death upon us, and had received power over us, might pass over us and do us no harm. Paul, 1 Cor. 5, refers to this so beautifully: "For even Christ our Passover is sacrificed for us," that we might be partakers of His blood, and that Satan, death and sin might have no authority over us and no power to do us hurt. This it is that John wishes us to learn here from his statement that Christ, like the paschal lamb, had no bone broken.

We would, however, consider here also the other particulars which the Jews had to observe with reference to the passover, so that when we see how perfectly the passover harmonizes with Christ, we may find more consolation in this sacrifice made for us, and take greater interest in the Lord Jesus.

The lamb was required to be without blemish, a male of the first year, healthy and strong; no other lamb would have answered the purposes of the passover. Now, as lambs one year old are very prolific, so this Lamb, the Lord Jesus, brought forth and built up His Church. The Lord Jesus is also without all blemish and deficiency, for He is the Son of God, and His flesh and blood is not sinful like ours, but He is holy altogether.

The Jews were directed to take the lamb from the sheep, or from the goats, on the tenth day of the month, and to keep it by itself until the fourteenth day of the month. In this way Christ was taken from the fold of God, that is, from the Jews, who were God's people, and for this reason He is called the Son of Abraham, or of David. He was separated for the special office of preaching God's kingdom among His people, the Jews, during the four years preceding His passion.

That the lamb had to be eaten in the evening, indicates that Christ should come in the latter times, when the Jews were no longer to be the people of God, and when the law and ceremonies of Moses were to cease. It is for this reason that the Lord sometimes compared His Gospel to a supper, and that the Apostles called the days of the New Testament "the latter times" and "the last days."

The lamb dared not to be eaten sodden or raw, but roasted. Throughout all Scripture, fire is an emblem of suffering and affliction. The lamb roasted with fire is, therefore, a type of Christ, who suffered death upon the cross. We dare not partake of Him raw, that is, he who would receive Him at all, dare not be careless, secure and profane as our Epicureans are, who think that they can believe and do as they please, and still be good Christians. These do not partake of the lamb properly, and cannot do so any more than they can who eat it sodden with water, that is, they who do not keep the doctrine pure, but adulterate it with human teachings and traditions, as the Pope does.

Unleavened bread and bitter herbs had to be eaten with the lamb. Thus Paul says: "Let us keep the feast, not with old leaven," refusing to check sin and to amend our conduct; "neither with the leaven of malice and wickedness," dealing in hypocrisy and not heartily repenting; "but with the unleavened bread of sincerity," keeping a clear conscience and living in the fear of God; "and truth," sincerely, not hypocritically, asking God's blessing and earnestly desiring to regulate ourselves according to His Word. This is the unleavened bread.

The herbs signify the holy cross; for, as Paul says: "All that will live godly in Christ Jesus shall suffer persecution."

No part of the lamb was allowed to remain, but the whole of it had to be eaten, or else that which remained was to be burned with fire. Neither should a bone of it be broken. Just so it is with Christ. He who would be a true Christian dares not eat one part and leave another part uneaten. He must accept and believe everything that Christ says, and must not, like the fanatics and sects, eat His words piecemeal. Arius was satisfied with everything else, only he would not believe that Christ was eternal God. The Anabaptists reject the baptism of children, despise this, the original institution, and fancy that they have found a better. The Sacramentarians of the present day accept everything Christ says, and think themselves excellent Christians. But it is not to their liking that Christ said, when He took the bread, "Take, eat; this is my body," and when He took the cup, "Drink ye all of it; for this is my blood of the New Testament," and this they do not want to believe. They do not like the taste of this and so they leave it uneaten, in spite of God's command that the whole of this Paschal Lamb should be eaten, or else the remainder burned with fire. And more than this, they even break the bones, that is, torture, crucify and mangle at pleasure the Word of the Lord Jesus, only so that they may give their scandalous error some plausibility. Thus we find that the Pope, the

Anabaptists, the Sacramentarians and, in short, all the sects, eat only that part of the lamb that suits their taste, and let the parts that they do not relish remain, and break them to pieces.

What must be done with the blood has already been related, viz., the blood of the Lamb is to pre vent sin, death and hell from hurting us, and, for all time to come, to hinder Pharaoh and the Egyptians, that is, Satan and the world, from oppressing and subduing us. Christ was sacrificed that He might make us free, John 8, and undo and destroy the work of Satan.

Of all this John would remind us when he says: "These things were done that the Scripture should be fulfilled, A bone of Him shall not be broken." He wishes us to regard the passover as the faithful picture of the entire benefit and of the real fruit of our Lord Jesus' sufferings. He wishes us to see that Christ was sacrificed for us and that His blood is to deliver us from sin, death and the devil, which constantly oppress, alarm and coerce us in the same way in which Pharaoh retained and vexed the children of Israel in Egypt. The blood of our Paschal Lamb, Christ Jesus, has abolished this servitude. We now have peace, and, fully free from every burden, we shall pass from dangerous Egypt over to the land of promise and to life eternal.

We shall now consider the third point, which the Evangelist evidently regarded as very important. He not only introduces the testimony of the Prophet Zechariah, who had prophesied concerning this piercing of Christ's side; but he also uses many and solemn words to affirm the miracle, that blood and water flowed from the dead body. This was unnatural, because when a man is dead his blood is cold and does not flow; and it was still more unnatural for both blood and water to flow from a corpse. Therefore John says: "He that saw it bare record, ... and he knoweth that he saith true, that ye might believe." He thus calls our attention to this miracle as one of great importance, so that we might diligently study it and finally learn from it to believe; that is, that we might through Christ and His death, as was said above when speaking of the passover, have the hope of the forgiveness of sins and of everlasting life. This is the chief design of this narrative as given by the Evangelist, with whom, as we shall soon see, the prophet completely corresponds.

First of all, however, let us rid ourselves of the idea that it was merely a casual circumstance that one of the soldiers thrust his spear into the corpse's side. The soldier, of course, did this in ignorance of any exalted signification the act might have. Still it was done by God's special arrangement, else the Holy Spirit would not have prophesied concerning it through Zechariah so many centuries before. We see that the Lord retained the wounds in His body after the resurrection, and that He showed them to His disciples in particular as a mark by which they might recognize Him. This piercing of Christ's side and this gushing forth of blood and water were not, therefore, mere accidents, but they were intended to mean and to accomplish something.

We must here be on our guard, lest we imitate the example commonly set by rude people, who say: It is none of my business what flowed from the Lord Jesus' side; it is enough for me to know that He died on the cross. Let us not think in this way, but let us honor the Holy Ghost and contribute to our own comfort by carefully learning what was accomplished by this piercing of Christ's side with the spear, which John so faithfully relates and which Zechariah had foretold so long before.

In the first place, it is certain beyond all dispute, that it is unnatural for a deceased body to sweat or bleed. As soon as blood grows cold it no longer flows, but it stagnates. The dead body before us now, however, is different foom all other dead bodies, and hence things take place in it that do not take place in any other body. True, Christ's body was flesh and blood like our own, and it died as ours must die. Yet, His flesh and blood were sinless, and therefore He died in such a way that even in His death a sign of life remained. The blood in all other bodies is soon cold and stagnant, but in the body of the Lord Jesus it remains so warm and active that, as soon as His side is pierced, it rushes forth as from a living body's opened vein. John wishes us to observe this carefully, and to learn from it that it is the true nature of the blood of our dear Lord Jesus to flow and live and be efficacious even after He has died. Neither was the blood of the paschal lamb used while the lamb lived, but after it was dead and had been eaten. The angel went by night through Egypt and smote all the first-born, but the houses of the Jews which were marked with the blood of the lamb he spared, and in them smote none. And thus the blood of our dear Lord Jesus continues still to live and flow, having neither become stagnant nor grown cold. It flows and gushes after He is dead, and all who are sprinkled with it have the forgiveness of sin and are children of eternal life.

We should mark this well, for this unnatural flowing shows that the blood of our dear Lord Jesus, as that of the true Paschal Lamb, retained its influence and power and virtue even after Christ's death; that it should flow upon, sprinkle and mark the faithful standing by the cross; and that Satan, death and sin should let alone all upon whom they find this mark, and not have power to hurt them. Such is the true nature, power and virtue of the blood of our dear Lord Jesus Christ, and such it forever remains in His Church even after His death.

Besides the blood, however, water also came out of Christ's side. This, no doubt, was to serve as an indication that the blood of Christ would sprinkle only those who were baptized in His name. Our Lord Jesus Himself says: "He that believeth and is baptized shall be saved; but he that believeth not shall be damned." Blood and water go together. Where Christ's blood is and operates, there the water of blessed Baptism also is; but where the water does not flow, that is, where there is no holy Baptism, there the blood of Christ is also wanting, nor does it flow there nor sprinkle any one, as it is the case among the Turks and Jews and heathen. Evermore must blood and water flow on together, and neither be separated from the other.

We must mark this well, for it has great value. It is not of great import for those who died under the Old Testament and who did not live to see Baptism; for they had their own Baptism and were saved by faith in the blessed Seed. Nor is it so important on account of infants who die in their mother's womb before they can be brought to Baptism; for their parents and the Christian assistants of those in travail bring to Christ the offering of fervent prayer in the hour of danger, and they are, without a doubt, accepted graciously. But the value of this token of mercy is our own, and we should not despise it and not prevent ourselves nor our families from accepting it. Where the water of this Baptism is, there too must be the blood of Christ, for water and blood come from His side together; and we have already seen the value of this blood, viz., it defends us against the destroying angel, cleanses us from sin, and causes us to live forever. The prophet, in such perfect harmony with the Evangelist, beautifully indicates this in Zech. 12, where he says: "I will pour upon the house of David, and upon the inhabitants of Jerusalem, the Spirit of grace and of supplications: and they shall look upon me whom they have pierced, and they shall mourn for Him, as one mourneth for his only son, and shall be in bitterness for Him, as one that is in bitterness for his first-born."

It cannot be denied, in the first place, that the prophet here speaks of the time of the New Testament and of the grace which should come upon us through the death of Christ. This grace, moreover, consists in God's pouring upon us "the Spirit of grace and of supplication," that is, God, through His Holy Spirit, brings comfort to our souls, so that we trust in His mercy and compassion through Christ, and call upon Him in every time of need, and seek help from Him, as children seek help from their father.

In the second place, John here throws upon us the light of his true apostolic spirit, when he says that the piercing, of which the prophet proceeds to speak, was done on the occasion of the crucifixion. The prophet tells us what shall be the result of this piercing, in these words: "They," mark you, they who have the Spirit of grace and of supplications,—"They shall look upon me whom they have pierced, and they shall mourn for Him, as one mourneth for his only son, and shall be in bitterness for Him, as one that is in bitterness for his first-born. This mourning and this bitterness mean nothing else than the thorough recognition of the sins for whose sake Christ suffered on the cross. Our looking upon Him who is pierced and our mourning for Him and our being sorrowful, indicates that He is innocent and that He suffered all for us.

His suffering thus, however, causes us to perceive our danger and distress, to desist from carelessly participating with the world in sin, to deplore our sinful heart and wicked life, to ask God for forgiveness, and to cling to the sufferings of Christ and console ourselves with them because He, being holy and obedient, did not deserve to die, but still took upon Himself and suffered death because He loved us so unspeakably.

It is necessary for us that we should pity, mourn and lament in the way stated above, and it is necessary for Christ to have our sympathy, grief and tears, or else He can have no Christian Church. The Church alone, as Zechariah says, looks upon the wounded Christ and weeps for Him, but not like the women at Jerusalem, for they wept for Christ in such a way as to overlook themselves. The tears of the believers, of the Christian Church, flow because the sins are seen within them, for which Christ suffered death.

Thus the prophet plainly points out to us the fruits of Christ's sufferings. And soon after, in the 13. chapter, he says: "In that day there shall be a fountain opened to the house of David and to the inhabitants of Jerusalem for sin and for uncleanness."

How closely the prophet unites the spear-thrust and the fountain, that is, the blood and the water, or holy Baptism. Now, if we would interpret this narrative correctly, we must say: Blood flows from the Lord Jesus' side for the washing away and forgiveness of my sins. The Lord Himself testifies to this when He takes the cup in the Holy Supper. But water also comes forth to show that His body is an open fountain. But why is it such? "For sin and for uncleanness." Baptism applies to us the blood of our Lord Jesus, for which reason Paul expresses this by saying, we are baptized into Christ's death, that is, we are baptized that the death of Christ might be our own and for our good, so that, being delivered from sin and death, we might live forever.

The holy fathers say some beautiful things about this. Augustine says that John uses the word "pierced,"—"One of the soldiers with a spear pierced His side,"—to show that the door of life was thus thrown open as it were, through which door came to us the holy Sacraments of the Church, without which Sacraments it is impossible to enter into that life which is the real life. He speaks of Sacraments, in the plural, because he refers not only to Baptism, which is represented by the water, but also to the Holy Supper, in which we drink Christ's blood. Chrysostom speaks after the same manner, saying: Whereas the sacred Mysteries here take their origin, thou must approach the holy Cup as if thou wast about to drink from the Lord Jesus' side.

The Sacramentarians dare not quote this passage of Chrysostom, for they boast that the whole of the old Church believed as they do, viz., that in the Lord's Supper there are only bread and wine, and not the body and blood of Christ. Now, how does this boast harmonize with the words of Chrysostom? They surely cannot be so blind and frantic as to say that wine flowed from Christ's side, and yet they say that in the Holy Supper we do not drink the blood of Christ, but merely wine. They must admit, on the testimony of Chrysostom, who says, thou must approach the holy Cup as if thou wast about to drink from Christ's side, that the ancient Church discerned not only wine, but also blood, in the Sacrament of the altar.

It is this flowing of both water and blood from Christ's side, that is said to have given rise to the custom of mixing the wine used in the Supper of the Lord with water. Cyprian vigorously defends this custom as a special ordinance of Christ, and the Armenians were condemned as heretics for not complying with it. Since Christ, however, did not command this to be done, and since the words of the institution tell us merely that Christ took the cup and gave it to His disciples, it is not necessary to hold this custom as essential.

We therefore let this matter rest and confine ourselves to the doctrine taught us by the holy Evangelist, which is, that the blood of our dear Lord Jesus Christ shall forever retain its power and efficacy after Christ's death, and shall preserve us from death and sin, provided we are baptized with water as Christ commanded. In Baptism we find the blood of Christ in reality, even as blood and water flow together here. Where the blood is, there is the water also, and where the water is, there also is the blood, and it accomplishes its purpose, which is to wash away our sins and to make us perfectly clean, even as Zechariah says when he prophesies concerning the open fountain "for sin and for uncleanness."

We should, therefore, thank God for the ineffable mercy and compassion, by which He has led us to this fountain, to be baptized in the name of His Son, and thus to be cleansed from our sins in the blood of Jesus Christ. We may now hope, through the Spirit of grace, to receive from God all good things, and can now call upon God in every hour of need, through the Spirit of supplications. And the final blessing of Christ's death shall come upon us in the end, when we leave this world of sorrows and enter life eternal. May God bestow this upon every one of us. Amen.

13

Christ's Body Taken down from the Cross and Laid in a Tomb.— The Soldiers Guard the Tomb

As evening approached, there came a rich man from Arimathea, named Joseph, who had himself become a disciple of Jesus. Going to Pilate, he asked for Jesus' body, and Pilate ordered that it be given to him. Joseph took the body, wrapped it in a clean linen cloth, and placed it in his own new tomb that he had cut out of the rock. He rolled a big stone in front of the entrance to the tomb and went away. Mary Magdalene and the other Mary were sitting there opposite the tomb. The next day, the one after Preparation Day, the chief priests and the Pharisees went to Pilate. "Sir," they said, "we remember that while he was still alive that deceiver said, 'After three days I will rise again.' So give the order for the tomb to be made secure until the third day. Otherwise, his disciples may come and steal the body and tell the people that he has been raised from the dead. This last deception will be worse than the first." "Take a guard," Pilate answered. "Go, make the tomb as secure as you know how." So they went and made the tomb secure by putting a seal on the stone and posting the guard.

—**MATTHEW 27:57–66.**

The concluding events related in the history of the sufferings of our Lord Jesus are His removal from the cross, His being laid in a new tomb, and the guarding of the tomb by the soldiers. And a most appropriate conclusion this is; for it shows how the death of our dear Lord Jesus influences both His friends and His enemies. His enemies become uneasy and apprehensive, and they perceptibly sink deeper into sin. They, however, who honestly love the Lord Jesus, are made confident and bold by the death of Christ, notwithstanding their weakness and timidity, and now venture to do what before they would not have thought of doing. The death of our dear Lord Jesus has just the same effect on men in our day, as we shall soon hear.

The shameful death of Christ upon the cross was indeed a most severe offence. Hence His foes blaspheme Him to the utmost, while His disciples, who had been about Him, did not dare to show themselves, and had no other thought than that all was over with Him now. His mother, the dear Virgin Mary, stood there distressed and full of sorrow, and other women with her. Now, although she closely kept in her heart the saying of the angel, and pondered the prophecies spoken by pious and holy people, such as the aged Simeon and Anna, a prophetess, when Jesus was yet a child, Luke 2, her affliction still overwhelmed her so and the offence so wounded her heart, that she could not speak. Thus the small assembly that had hitherto adhered to Christ and kept Him company is perfectly mute. The condemned malefactor is the only one who moves or speaks. Christ's enemies carry the day and are full of hope and gladness. The clamor made is all their own, the rest must hold their peace.

The weakness and timidity of these pious people serves, as said above, to teach us not to be rash and not to place too much reliance in ourselves. If these almost lose sight of comfort and are swallowed up, as it were, by grief and misery, how much more shall not we be subject to such weakness when called upon to expose ourselves or to suffer for the Gospel's sake. How very necessary, therefore, that we should abide in the fear of God and pray for the Holy Spirit, that He may enlighten and comfort our hearts, and make us bold enough to dare and to bear something for the glory of God and for the sake of His Word.

When the offence was at its very height, and when they who had been the best Christians and had fearlessly clung to the Lord Jesus began to falter and to shrink, and, on account of fear, sorrow and gloom, knew not what to do nor whither to go, the first to approach was Joseph of Arimathea, a city which is also called Arumah, Joshua 15 and Judges 9. Joseph was not a plain and common citizen, like the Apostles, who were simply common people, but he was a member of the council of Jerusalem and very rich. He it was who ventured to go to Pilate and beg for the dead body, that he might take it down from the cross and bury it. And then came also Nicodemus, who, although he loved the Lord and His Word, had been so timorous that he came to Him only by night. He brought about a hundred pounds of myrrh and aloes, so that the Lord might not be buried meanly, but with honor. It was customary among the Jews, as John relates, because they had derived from the Word of God the hope of the resurrection and of everlasting life, to give the bodies of the deceased a decent burial by preparing them with myrrh and aloes, so that they would not only be preserved for a long time and decay slowly, but also that they would have an agreeable odor.

Mark and Luke specially mention that Joseph was a disciple of Christ, that is, he attentively and approvingly heard Christ preach, and waited for the kingdom of God. We must carefully bear this in mind, for from this we learn what prompted him to have the boldness to go to Pilate, which was not a trifling matter.

The chief priests and the entire council at Jerusalem had accused the Lord Jesus as a perverter of the nation, as a deceiver and blasphemer, and on this accusation Pilate based his judgment. Now, Joseph, who had taken no part in any of the proceedings against the Lord Jesus and did not want to be present at His trial, did a very dangerous thing when he sought Christ's body for a decent burial. He was thus likely to incur the fury of the whole council and of Pilate himself, who had condemned the Lord, and he thus gave them to understand that in his opinion Christ had been a pious and a good Man, who had been wronged in the sight of God and the world.

What moved him so boldly to expose himself? Only this, he was waiting for the kingdom of God. That is, he still believed that God's kingdom would not fail to come, and that Christ, although He had so miserably hung and died upon the cross, would be raised from the dead by God, and that He would accomplish and furnish everything necessary to fulfill the prophesies concerning the Messiah and his kingdom. If the centurion who stood over against Him and saw Christ die when He had cried with a loud voice, learned so much from various occurrences, such as the darkness and the earthquake, that he openly confessed: "Truly this Man was the Son of God," how much more would not this Joseph and pious Nicodemus also have had such thoughts! Without a doubt, the preaching of the prophets, and the words of Christ which they had repeatedly heard and which they had now, through the admonition of the Holy Spirit, taken to heart for the first time, conveyed to them the hope that Christ had not been finally disposed of, but that God would establish His kingdom now when men least looked for it. Christ had, for instance, preached to Nicodemus a powerful sermon on this hope, telling him, John 3, that as the serpent was lifted up in the wilderness so He also would be lifted up on the cross.

The Holy Spirit, at that time, kindled such thoughts in their weak and timid hearts, which soon influenced them so that Joseph goes to Pilate and asks for the body of Him whom Pilate had condemned as a disturber and blasphemer. Nicodemus brings myrrh and aloes, with which to give the Lord a costly and decent burial, as their testimony before all the world that they yet hoped that God's kingdom still would come, although defied by Jerusalem's haughtiest boast that Christ was gone and things would soon be changed.

Such is the fruit of our dear Lord Jesus' death. The weakest and most diffident distinguish themselves by boldly and fearlessly confessing Christ and by asking for His body, which hangs in the greatest disgrace, that they might bury it with the greatest honor. They thus testify that they, in spite of Jews, chief priests, Pilate, and all foes of Christ, regard and glorify Christ as the Son of God, hope for His kingdom, and find comfort in Him even now when He is dead and when every body thinks that He is gone forever. This is exactly as Mark and Luke say: Joseph "waited for the kingdom of God," that is, he hoped that God, through this Man, would found a new kingdom on the earth, forgive sins, and impart the Holy Spirit and eternal life. For, according to the prophets, the great, essential feature of God's kingdom is, that Christ, or the Messiah, must establish it.

Isaiah's prophecy concerning Christ, "A bruised reed shall He not break, and the smoking flax shall He not quench," is here fulfilled in the case of Joseph and Nicodemus. Hitherto they were weak and timid Christians. They suffered much from their fear, which prevented them from making an open confession. It is for this reason that John speaks of Nicodemus, who came to Jesus by night, as a secret disciple. Christ forgave them this fear, and did not cast them away on account of it. Now, however, when the danger is greatest and when they who usually were such strong and bold

Christians are overcome by the offence, and fear to let themselves be seen, the Holy Spirit, through the death of Christ, fans the smoking and nearly smothered flax until it makes a blaze as bright as the beautiful sun. What Joseph had so far been thinking and believing of Christ in secret, he now makes known to all, fearing neither the Jews nor Pilate. He cares more for Christ, who died in the deepest disgrace, than for all the world. Let us not regard this as insignificant, or as a mere result of Christ's sufferings. These things are written as examples for us all, that we should imitate Joseph and Nicodemus. When Christ hangs on the cross, that is, when the Gospel is persecuted and poor Christians are tortured for its sake, we should stand forth, and, not heeding the tyrant's wrath, glorify God's Son and His Word, and honor it by publicly confessing it until Christ who died shall appear in His glorious resurrection, when faint-hearted, timid, and fearful Christians also shall receive comfort and return to the confession.

Such changes shall always occur in the Church. Some are offended and fall back, and generally the strongest grow weak when affliction comes, while the weakest advance and let their joyful confession be heard, so that there are always some who acknowledge and confess Christ. Whether it is unwillingness or inability that keeps the strong from doing this, on account of the offence, the very weakest, who make no display at all, must do it for them, and the former then learn and experience the utter nothingness of men when God removes His Spirit from them. God, as a rich Householder, wants all kinds of servants in His house; not only such as are strong and full grown, but also such as are weak and small. That the strong may not despise the rest, they have occasion given them to see weakness in themselves; and that no one may judge his fellow, God's Spirit comes upon the weak, admonishing, comforting and strengthening them in such measure that all must see and praise God's power in them. The sufferings of our dear Lord Jesus operate thus in His Church forever, in order that it may not go to ruin, but stand and grow and expand.

What, however, is the effect on those who hate the Lord Jesus, and who have no peace until they have crucified Him? Just the reverse. The effect of Christ's death can be compared to the effect of the sun, which is different on different materials. Wax is softened and melted by the sun, while mud is made hard and dry. Pious hearts are made so cheerful and bold by the sufferings of Christ, that they venture to do what they would by no means have attempted while Christ yet lived.

The godless Jews hurried Christ off to death in the hope that, when He should have been silenced, their cares would forever be gone. But when their malice was gratified in seeing that Christ had died upon the cross and was laid into a new tomb, they begin to be uneasy, and they all go to Pilate and say:

"Sir, we remember that that deceiver said, while He was yet alive, After three days I will rise again. Command therefore that the sepulchre be made sure until the third day, lest His disciples come by night, and steal Him away, and say unto the people, He is risen from the dead: so the last error shall be worse than the first."

If we carefully notice these words we shall find what kind of hearts these people had. They remembered Christ's sayings well enough and understood them too, but what fruit did His sayings bring forth in them? Joseph and Nicodemus, who, no doubt, also remembered these words and comforted themselves with them at the time they were spoken, are now made courageous and joyful by them, and hope for every blessing. But these knaves grow restless, and begin to get scared at the dead Man, however natural it may otherwise be for men not to fear an enemy after they know him to be dead. The wicked Jews enjoy no such composure, but, as we see, they fear the departed Christ, who is lying in the tomb.

Before Pilate they pretended that His disciples might steal Him away and say that He is risen; but in their hearts the words of the Lord Jesus are such a pricking and piercing thorn that they anxiously ask themselves: What if they were true after all? What if He should be the Messiah and rise again from the dead? What would become of us then?—This disturbs and disheartens them. But they are none the better for these thoughts. They do not argue thus: Alas, what have we done! Let us yet creep to the cross and not despise the excellent admonitions and miracles which came to light at His death.—No, they do not want to think in this way. They persist in that hatred and enmity with which they persecuted the Lord Jesus. They perceptibly grow worse and more wicked still. They devise all possible means and ways for annihilating the Lord Jesus and for diminishing His glory.

This too was written as an example and warning for us, that, when we see similar things done by the enemies of the Word, we may not become frightened. God's inevitable rule is this: the longer a man willfully opposes the Word, the deeper he must sink into sin, and the longer he seeks rest, the greater shall grow his restlessness and fear. It was just so too in the case of the blood of the Lord Jesus, of which we heard above. The Jews thought it a very little thing that they nailed Christ to the cross and slew Him. In a deliberate, careless and trifling spirit they say: "His blood be on us, and on our children." They afterward found what a little thing it was, alas, for Jerusalem and the whole land to be ruined on account of this. Here the case is exactly as it was there. They thought: If only this Jesus were out of the way once, we should not be troubled any more. Now, in the 2. chapter of Acts it is written that Christ was "delivered by the determinate counsel and foreknowledge of God" into the shameful death upon the cross. This only increased the fears of the Jews, so that they had less peace than before. The words of Christ, although they did not believe them, still lay in their hearts like a burning fire, or a gnawing worm. While they could not believe them, they still could not altogether set them aside. So it must always be with the foes of the Word. The more they seek peace by means of tyranny, the deeper they fall, not only into trouble, but also into sin.

Although their plans may be laid in the greatest wisdom, they shall find in the end that they have only injured their cause, and aided the Gospel in spite of themselves, just as it was with the Jews. These demanded guards of Pilate, who should make the sepulchre sure until the third day. "Pilate said unto them, Ye have a watch: go your way, make it as sure as ye can." Matthew says, "They went and made the sepulchre sure, sealing the stone, and setting a watch." This they did to prevent the disciples from stealing the body of the Lord Jesus and from telling the people that Christ was risen from the dead. It was very wisely schemed, but how did it succeed? Their very fears were realized. When, early on Easter morning, Christ had risen from the dead, and the angel descended from heaven and came to the sepulchre and rolled back the stone from the door, and a great earthquake came, the keepers did shake, and became as dead men. As soon as they had recovered from the shock, they gathered themselves up, one ran this way, another that, and came to Jerusalem, where they told the chief priests all the things that were done. What, think you, must then have been the thoughts of these priests? How must their hearts not have quaked and trembled! They could not look on it as a jest, for there stood their own witnesses, the soldiers of Pilate, whom Pilate himself had sent to guard the tomb. These not only told them, but also showed in their entire conduct, what had happened. So severe a fright as theirs had been, is not so easily concealed. The speech betrays it; the countenance shows it; the whole body is so affected by it, as to make it known. It is, therefore, easily seen that this message must have terribly frightened the chief priests and elders.

Instead, however, of being bettered by this message, they only rushed deeper into sin and made their evil conscience worse. They held a council on that very Sabbath day, and gave much money to the soldiers that they might help them lie, and instructed them to say, "His disciples came by night, and stole Him away while we slept." In this way these poor fellows sought to console and help themselves. They believed in their hearts that Christ, whom they had delivered to die, though innocent, had risen from the dead. Each one can imagine for himself how this must have troubled them; for, under such circumstances, their hearts could never have been calm. And yet, they gave much money to have their lies spread, and to have people persuaded to believe what they themselves did not believe. They who thus willfully resist the truth, and adorn and comfort themselves with known falsehoods, are surely spiteful and desperate wretches. We should learn this, so that we may know how to look upon the foes of the Word. He who resists the truth, as has been said already, has only falsehood left to shield him.

In the meanwhile our dear Lord Jesus comforts His few scattered followers, and shows Himself to them, and proves to them by very deed that He is not dead, but living, and living as the Conqueror of death forever. The lies of those who hate the Word only help so much the more to spread the tidings and to give them notoriety. Had the Jews not guarded the tomb themselves, the falsehood, that Christ's body had been stolen, would have been more plausible; but it does not serve its purpose; for the guards had been stationed around the tomb, and the door of the sepulchre had been carefully sealed. The very fact of their fleeing sufficiently shows that a higher and greater power than that of Pilate and his guards was present.

So it always is with the enemies of the Gospel. They must resort to base and blasphemous lies, which, however, do not harm the Word, but further it in spite of them. This should move every one to learn to know and to flee from lies, and to abide by the Word and by the truth. God be praised that some in our day have learned this, and that the Papists only advanced the cause of the Gospel with their lying and clamoring and scribbling! Their lies are published in such clumsy shape that men are driven to the truth by them. The longer the enemies of the truth attack it, the more violent they become; but the suffering of our dear Lord Jesus has brought it about that they must thus, against their will, further the truth.

www.ingramcontent.com/pod-product-compliance
Lightning Source LLC
Chambersburg PA
CBHW031445040426
42444CB00007B/983